THE FILMS OF THE

by Jerry Vermilye

The Citadel Press

TWENTIES

Secaucus, New Jersey

Library of Congress Cataloging-in-Publication Data

Vermilye, Jerry.
    The films of the twenties.

    1. Moving-pictures—United States—Plots, themes,
etc.   I. Title.
PN1997.8.V45   1985   791.43′75′0973   85-13289
ISBN 0-8065-0960-0

Published by Citadel Press
A division of Lyle Stuart Inc.
120 Enterprise Ave., Secaucus, N.J. 07094
In Canada: Musson Book Company
A division of General Publishing Co. Limited
Don Mills, Ontario
DESIGNED BY LESTER GLASSNER

Queries regarding rights and permissions should be
addressed to: Lyle Stuart, 120 Enterprise Avenue,
Secaucus, N.J. 07094

Manufactured in the United States of America

ACKNOWLEDGMENTS

The author would like to thank the following individuals and organizations who variously helped arrange screenings, made possible the acquisition of unusual stills or otherwise aided in informational research:

The British Film Institute's National Film Archive, Danny Burk, Judy and Paul Caputo, Mary Corliss and the Museum of Modern Art's Film Stills Archive, Harry Forbes, Dolores and Al Kilgore, Harold Kinkaid, Franklyn Lenthall and the Boothbay Theatre Museum, Mark Van Alstyne and Mark Ricci's Memory Shop.

With special thanks to Bob Finn and Allan Turner.

And a nod of gratitude to the companies which distributed these movies and employed the anonymous still photographers whose artistry preserved the images in this volume: Chadwick Pictures, First National/Warner Bros., Fox Film Corp., W.W. Hodkinson Corp., Metro-Goldwyn-Mayer, Paramount Pictures, Producers Distributing Corp., United Artists and Universal Pictures.

With a final note of appreciation for the efforts of those distinguished film archaeologists whose considerable scholarship has already told us so much about the movies of the Twenties: DeWitt Bodeen, Kevin Brownlow, Homer C. Dickens, William K. Everson, Ephraim Katz, George C. Pratt, David Robinson, David Shipman, Jack Spears, Edward Wagenknecht and Alexander Walker.

ALSO BY JERRY VERMILYE

For

Marjorie and Lay
—who were there

and for

Connie
—who wasn't

Lillian Gish

CONTENTS

Greta Garbo

Nancy Carroll

AUTHOR'S INTRODUCTION

Encompassing an entire decade of Hollywood filmmaking in a single volume that covers only seventy-five motion pictures inevitably means that there are bound to be some important omissions, of title as well as performer. But, as with *The Films of the Thirties*, the author's intent was not merely to celebrate the acknowledged classics of the era, although a representation of those will indeed be found within these pages. Rather, it is the *essence* of those prosperous ten years that fell between the end of the "Great War" and the Stock Market Crash of October, 1929, that concerns us here. A handful of producers and directors such as D. W. Griffith, Thomas Ince, Cecil B. DeMille, Mack Sennett and Erich von Stroheim were recognizable names to the general moviegoing public. But it was mostly an age of *stars*, whose collective aura of glamorous magnetism—along with the talents to amuse, move, inspire, attract or distract the public—kept moviegoing a popular habit in an age that could scarcely have anticipated the home-competition that would one day arise from television.

In retrospect, it seems difficult to understand why the coming of sound at the end of the Twenties spelled doom for so many of the major silent stars. It was as though the movie moguls had been mass-ordered to clean their houses of proven silent-screen talent, except for that collection of Broadway-trained actors whose film careers burgeoned as the Twenties waned, and start casting from a clean slate. And inadequate speaking voices were not always the reason. Some stars, of course, were justifiably afraid of what the microphone would reveal of their vocal shortcomings. But for many others, those fears were unfounded. Not a few silent favorites like Mary Pickford, Douglas Fairbanks, Lillian Gish, Billie Dove, Harold Lloyd, Betty Bronson, Bebe Daniels, Charles Farrell, Colleen Moore, Nancy Carroll, Richard Barthelmess and Clara Bow made the vocal transition with ease, but found their careers declining for other reasons. With some, the problem was middle-age and the fickleness of a public that had become more interested in the newer and younger stars that were emerging with the early talkies. For others, ill-chosen vehicles hastened their retirement or moved them to seek new careers on the stage or in the increasingly popular medium of radio.

Untimely death claimed the lives of two of the Twenties' top stars, Lon Chaney and Milton Sills, just as they were proving themselves—in their late forties—capable of continued success in the sound medium. But careers like those of Joan Crawford, Norma Shearer, Ronald Colman, Myrna Loy, Gary Cooper, Janet Gaynor and William Powell would continue to flourish and fulfill the promise that they had held in the Twenties. Silent starlets

Douglas Fairbanks Jr. and Billie Dove in "WILD HORSE MESA"

like Jean Arthur, Loretta Young, Jean Harlow and Carole Lombard would soon blossom forth as popular leading ladies of the Thirties, while "old reliables" like Richard Dix, Warner Baxter, Wallace Beery, Lionel Barrymore and Lewis Stone would become even more reliable with the power of their voices. But many were the silent stars who elected for early retirement while still in their late twenties or early thirties, leaving the silver screen before they could legitimately be called "has-beens." Less prescient performers chose to stick it out in that shaky Depression Era when circumstances saw many a contract end, and where the only available roles were in the low-budget "quickies" destined for the bottom half of a double-bill. In the Thirties, that's where moviegoers were most likely to find such competent Twenties players as Dorothy Mackaill, Betty Blythe, Lloyd Hughes, Esther Ralston, Anita Page, Claire Windsor, John Gilbert, Neil Hamilton, Sue Carol, Mary Brian, Jack Mulhall and Pauline Starke. Only a few brief years would spell the difference between mid-Twenties stardom at MGM, Paramount or First National and leading roles at "Poverty Row" studios like Tiffany, Liberty or Chesterfield during the early Thirties.

Since so many Twenties movies have been literally *lost* to the ravages of time by an industry once careless of any need to preserve past efforts, it's now difficult to evaluate *all* of that decade's considerable output. But recent years have seen a growing interest in film-restoration, as well as the availability of more than a few silent movies on videocassette, especially from the Iowa-based Blackhawk Films. And the recent issuance by Paramount of its 1927 *Wings*, the first Academy Award-winning Best Picture, and by MGM/UA of Greta Garbo's 1929 *Wild Orchids* indicate that somebody out there thinks there's still gold to be mined from the silents.

Janet Gaynor and Charles Farrell in "SEVENTH HEAVEN"

William Boyd and Mary Astor in "TWO ARABIAN KNIGHTS"

Loretta Young and Lon Chaney in "LAUGH, CLOWN, LAUGH"

Before directing the reader to this volume's collection of movies, it seems only fair to mention a few of the omissions. In May of 1929, when Hollywood first celebrated its own excellence with an Academy Awards ceremony honoring films of 1927-28 (they weren't yet known as "Oscars"), several citations went to the sensationally popular romantic drama *Seventh Heaven* (1927), which won awards for director Frank Borzage, actress Janet Gaynor and screenwriter Benjamin Glazer. That movie also established the "love team" of Gaynor and Charles Farrell, who would co-star opposite one another in twelve additional films between 1927 and 1934. An unusual Academy Award category that first year—and *only* that year—was "Comedy Directing," for which Lewis Milestone took home a statuette representing 1927's now-nearly-forgotten *Two Arabian Knights*, in which Louis Wolheim and a pre-Hopalong Cassidy William Boyd played American soldiers who escaped from army imprisonment in Arab mufti. In her memoir *A Life on Film*, the movie's distaff star Mary Astor recalls it fondly.

Another of that first year's curious—and almost immediately obsolete—Academy Award categories was that of "Title Writing," which brought Joseph Farnham a statuette for his work on the 1928 *Laugh, Clown, Laugh*, a film once reputed to be the personal favorite of its star Lon Chaney. Chaney's leading lady in that one, incidentally, was a promising teen-ager named Loretta Young.

Warner Baxter and Dorothy Burgess in "IN OLD ARIZONA"

Wallace Reid and Gloria Swanson in ► "THE AFFAIRS OF ANATOL"

Monte Blue and Raquel Torres in "WHITE SHADOWS IN THE SOUTH SEAS"

Anthony Bushell, George Arliss and Joan Bennett in "DISRAELI"

*ZaSu Pitts and Gibson
Gowland in "GREED"*

*Harry Langdon and
Joan Crawford in
"TRAMP, TRAMP,
TRAMP"*

Mabel Normand

In the motion picture academy's second annual ceremony, which reflected films released during the 1928-29 season, thirty-nine-year-old Warner Baxter won Best Actor recognition for his Cisco Kid in the colorful Western *In Old Arizona*, and cameraman Clyde De Vinna copped an award for his brilliant location photography of 1928's *White Shadows in the South Seas*, in which Monte Blue and Raquel Torres headed an almost "all-native" cast.

In the academy's third competition, there were no less than eight nominations for Best Actor, including two each for Ronald Colman, Maurice Chevalier and George Arliss. The latter won his statuette for 1929's *Disraeli*, opposite a then-blonde, young Joan Bennett. But he lost for his 1930 remake of *The Green Goddess*, which Arliss had already played to perfection in 1923.

To dip further back into the Twenties, one notes a number of important stars whose careers were brought to an untimely end through personal misfortune or the type of scandal that nowadays would hardly affect an otherwise successful performer. But, in 1921,

Roland Young and John Barrymore in "SHERLOCK HOLMES"

comedian Roscoe "Fatty" Arbuckle (an audience favorite of the Teens) was ruined by the death of a partying starlet of whose sex-murder he was eventually acquitted—too late to rescue his reputation. Wallace Reid was a handsome and popular leading man who wrote, directed and starred in an impressive array of movies (*e.g., Double Speed, The Affairs of Anatol* and *Forever*) between 1910 and 1923, the year he died at thirty-two. Reid's sad, premature demise was chiefly attributable to the morphine that had first been administered to alleviate painful injuries incurred during a filming accident.

Saucer-eyed Mabel Normand has been called the silent screen's most brilliant comedienne, because of the pictures she made for Mack Sennett during the Teens. But her name was dragged into notoriety in two sensational murder cases of the early Twenties, and after that—with the possible exception of 1924's *The Extra Girl*—her career took a nose-dive. And so did Mabel's health, precipitating her death in 1930 of combined pneumonia and tuberculosis, when she was only thirty-five. Beautiful Barbara La Marr played the treacherous Milady de Winter in the popular 1921 Fairbanks version of *The Three Musketeers*, and continued to star in movies through 1926, the year she died of narcotics addiction at the age of twenty-nine. A similar fate claimed the life, in 1931, of the thirty-three-year-old Twenties star Alma Rubens, a dark-eyed beauty whose many films included *Humoresque* (1920) and *Showboat* (1929), in which she portrayed the tragic Julie.

Nor did the decade's great comedians all sustain the popular heights of a Chaplin, a Lloyd or a Keaton. Sad-eyed Harry Langdon, whose career reached its zenith with three excellent comedies of the later Twenties (*Tramp, Tramp, Tramp; The Strong Man; Long Pants*), became inflated by his own success, with unfortunate results. Raymond Griffith, a silent comedian capable of brilliance (the 1926 Civil War comedy *Hands Up!*) had no chance of surviving silent films as an actor because an earlier accident had so badly damaged his vocal chords that he could barely speak above a whisper.

ZaSu Pitts is fondly recalled by many for her general body of work as a comic actress of eccentric, fluttery mannerisms. But many recall her unexpectedly powerful excursion into serious acting as the unusual heroine of Erich von Stroheim's legendary 1924 *Greed*, a film almost more famous for what was *cut* from it than for what was shown in theatres. Equally celebrated today, although there are some who question the reverence in which it's held, is *A Woman of Paris*, the only silent Charlie Chaplin movie in which the comedian didn't also star.

Adolphe Menjou and Edna Purviance in "A WOMAN OF PARIS"

Leatrice Joy in "THE SILENT PARTNER"

Victor Varconi and Phyllis Haver in "CHICAGO"

Harold Lloyd in "SAFETY LAST"

It had been tailored for Chaplin's then-favorite leading lady, Edna Purviance, an uncharismatic blonde who came off less memorably than the film's suave male star Adolphe Menjou, whose career was thereafter wedded to fine manners and dinner clothes.

Roland Young was another character actor closely associated with lovably odd comic characters. But few remember that Young's movie career began in support of John Barrymore, playing a thoughtfully droll Dr. Watson to the matinee idol's *Sherlock Holmes* in 1922. Equally forgotten is Phyllis Haver, the beautiful blonde who began as a Mack Sennett bathing beauty in 1917 and ten years later scored as Roxie Hart, the brassy murder suspect of *Chicago*, before retiring from movies to wed a millionaire in 1929. Another silent star unsung in recent years is Leatrice Joy, that stylish leading lady of such Cecil B. DeMille epics as *Manslaughter* (1922) and *The Ten Commandments* (1923). By cutting her hair to a mannish bob, the actress sorely displeased the Great Director, but in so doing she set a trend that widely influenced not only the industry but also America's women.

Another influential trendsetter was Rudolph Valentino, an Italian emigrant who started as an extra in 1918 and, three years later, portrayed the sensuous title role opposite Agnes Ayres in a movie called *The Sheik* that had women literally fainting in the aisles in vicarious ecstasy. His legend could only increase when audiences flocked to see him in *The Four Horsemen of the Apocalypse* (1921) and *Blood and Sand* (1922).

Providing yet another kind of thrill for moviegoers was Harold Lloyd, whose reputation as a daredevil comic actor has been reinforced over the years by the many published photographs of him from silent classics like *Safety Last* (1923), in which he dangled from the hands of a clock on the wall of a tall city building. Since Lloyd did most of those stunts himself, it's all the more amazing to realize that the actor had injured his right hand in a 1920 filming accident, and thereafter worked minus a right thumb and forefinger, over which he wore a handlike glove to disguise his handicap.

The legend surrounding John Gilbert, one of the silent screen's most popular leading men, is that his career was ruined by a high, squeaky voice that belied his urbane, masculine image. In recent years, reports have surfaced to refute that canard, with one even going so far as to suggest that a violent run-in with his MGM boss, Louis B. Mayer, resulted in the mogul's

Rudolph Valentino and Agnes Ayres in "THE SHEIK"

deliberately sabotaging the sound recording on Gilbert's 1929 talkie debut in *His Glorious Night*, thus drawing unwanted audience laughter. Whatever the truth of this explanation, Gilbert's fine silent performance in King Vidor's 1925 World War I classic *The Big Parade*, opposite the piquant French actress Renée Adorée, remains as testimony to the actor's talent, as do those steamy 1927 romantic dramas with Garbo, *Flesh and the Devil* and *Love*.

Classic movies do not go unrepresented in this book, but neither are *all* the Twenties' best motion pictures covered here. Lon Chaney's unforgettable interpretation of *The Hunchback of Notre Dame* (1923) seems all the more remarkable when we know that he suffered with a hump-and-harness contraption that added seventy pounds to his costuming. To say nothing of that disfiguring horror makeup Chaney designed for the role!

In the Twenties, super-Westerns were not yet commonplace. But John Ford's 1924 railroad epic *The Iron Horse*, in which muscular George O'Brien and wispy Madge Bellamy occasionally found time for romance, was an important milestone, coming as it did a year after James Cruze's equally well-remembered *The Covered Wagon*. And, for less demanding outdoor-movie fans, there were always the program Westerns of Buck Jones, Hoot Gibson, Tom Mix, Ken Maynard, Fred Thomson, Tim McCoy, Bob Steele, Jack Hoxie and Art Acord, among others.

John Gilbert and Renee Adoree in "THE BIG PARADE"

Lars Hanson, Greta Garbo and John Gilbert in "FLESH AND THE DEVIL"

Nigel de Brulier and Lon Chaney in "THE HUNCHBACK OF NOTRE DAME" ▶

Lila Lee and Thomas Meighan in "COMING THROUGH"

Paul Muni and Marguerite Churchill in "THE VALIANT"

In 1926, Raoul Walsh's *What Price Glory* joined 1925's *The Big Parade* in popularity for audiences intrigued with tales of World War I, but the former movie included more comedy in its narrative, especially with regard to the rivalry of those battling sergeants Quirt and Flagg, as respectively portrayed by Edmund Lowe and Victor McLaglen. *What Price Glory* fostered a series of popular follow-up adventure films in which the two actors sustained that brawling relationship.

Among the early sound era's most popular and engaging personalities were a handful of Broadway-trained performers whose vivid individuality can scarcely be measured by today's actors. Thirty-four-year-old Paul Muni made an impressive enough screen debut in 1929's prison drama *The Valiant* to earn himself an Academy Award nomination, but it would be seven more years before he would win the statuette for *The Story of Louis Pasteur*. Others bringing their stage training to motion pictures as the screen found its voice included such luminaries as Claudette Colbert and Edward G. Robinson (*The Hole in the Wall*), Sylvia Sidney (*Thru Different Eyes*), Walter Huston (*The Lady Lies*) and Ruth Chatterton (*Sins of the Fathers*). Barbara Stanwyck, another 1929 newcomer from Broadway, had the female lead in a minor melodrama entitled *The Locked Door* that gave little promise of the three nominations she would later earn—or the belated 1982 Oscar given to Stanwyck for the overall achievements of her notable career.

George O'Brien and Madge Bellamy in "THE IRON HORSE"

Victor McLaglen, Dolores Del Rio and Edmund Lowe in "WHAT PRICE GLORY"

Barbara Stanwyck and William (Stage) Boyd in "THE LOCKED DOOR"

Before closing, it seems fitting to consider for a moment the film work of two unsung stars of yesteryear who typified the silent-to-sound era. Both Lila Lee and Thomas Meighan were popular performers from the Teens whose voices enabled them to traverse the Twenties into talkies with ease. Some of their best work was in the films they did together, such as DeMille's 1919 *Male and Female* and the 1925 drama *Coming Through*. They never became what we would now term "superstars," but both delivered work that was professional and reliable. Eventually, Lee left a dwindling film career for the stage in 1937, while Meighan continued to play leads until just two years before his death, at fifty-seven, in 1936. Today, nobody writes books about Lila Lee or Thomas Meighan or holds retrospectives in their names. But it was actors like these whose modest careers typified the Hollywood films of the silent era and formed the industry's backbone.

The movies surveyed in the pages that follow illustrate some of the trends and changes rung in during that ten-year period encompassed by Mary Pickford's little-girl performance of the title role in 1920's *Pollyanna* and her grown-up interpretation of Shakespeare's *The Taming of the Shrew* in 1929. This volume, then, can only hope to reflect some of the highlights—and even a few lowlights—of Hollywood's films of the Twenties, perhaps inspiring the curious reader to dig even deeper into the history of a sometimes foolish, often wonderful motion picture era that should not be neglected.

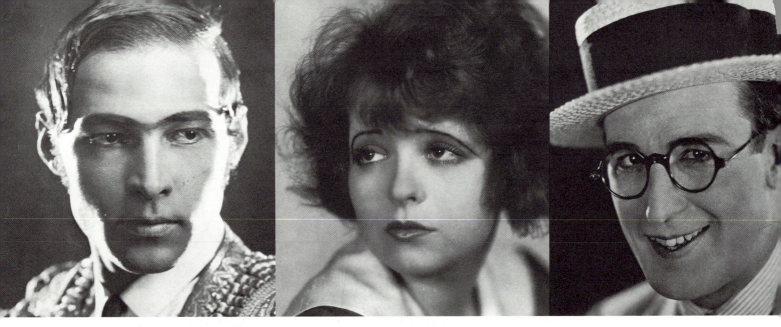

VALENTINO   CLARA BOW   HAROLD LLOYD

JOAN CRAWFORD   EVELYN BRENT   GARY COOPER

BETTY COMPSON   POLA NEGRI   ESTHER RALSTON

MARY ASTOR   JOHN GILBERT   LOUISE BROOKS

BARBARA LAMARR   LILLIAN GISH   RICHARD ARLEN

DOUGLAS FAIRBANKS JR.   MARY PICKFORD   GLORIA SWANSON

Mary Pickford

POLLYANNA

1920

CREDITS

A United Artists Picture. A Mary Pickford Co. Production. Directed by Paul Powell. Scenario by Frances Marion. Based on the novel by Eleanor H. Porter and the play by Catherine Chisholm Cushing. Photographed by Charles Rosher. Art Direction by Max Parker. Six reels.

CAST

Mary Pickford (*Pollyanna Whittier*); J. Wharton James (*Rev. John Whittier*); Katherine Griffith (*Aunt Polly Harrington*); Helen Jerome Eddy (*Nancy Thing*); George Berrell (*Old Tom*); Howard Ralston (*Jimmy Bean*); William Courtleigh (*John Pendleton*); Herbert Prior (*Dr. Chilton*).

In the Teens, Mary Pickford reigned supreme as "America's Sweetheart," a term that still dogged the long-retired actress at her death in 1979, age eighty-six. One of the film industry's true pioneers, Mary was Hollywood's first independent star-producer, as well as one of the four founding members of United Artists, along with Charlie Chaplin, Douglas Fairbanks and director D. W. Griffith. She was also among those helping to establish the Academy of Motion Picture Arts and Sciences in the late Twenties. In 1916, when she founded The Mary Pickford Co., this actress was the highest-paid performer in the industry.

Diminutive in stature and extremely youthful in appearance, Mary gained her fame as the screen's most delightful little girl, a persona that she nurtured even into her thirties, because that was how her public wished to see her. In 1919, when she filmed *Pollyanna*, Mary was already twenty-six. But to give her fans what they wanted, she maintained her long, golden curls and little-girl mannerisms—with only occasional forays into more adult roles such as *Stella Maris* (1918), *Rosita* (1923) and *Dorothy Vernon of Haddon Hall* (1924). It has been recorded that Mary Pickford hated the film *Pollyanna*, yet it more than satisfied the demands of her considerable public. And the movie's great success finally established the struggling United Artists.

The name "Pollyanna" long ago entered the language as a synonym for one who habitually harbors blind, unfounded optimism for herself as well as others by

Helen Jerome Eddy, Katherine Griffith, George Berrell, Mary Pickford, Herbert Prior and William Courtleigh

always "making the best of things." The original *Pollyanna* sprang from the imagination of Eleanor H. Porter, who created that child-heroine in a series of best-selling books for young people, and who died, aged fifty-two, in 1920, the very year Pickford brought *Pollyanna* to life on the screen. Four years earlier, Patricia Collinge had portrayed the perennially cheerful waif in a Broadway play that ran for 112 performances.

Pollyanna's rather sticky plot belongs to the sentimental past and fits uneasily on today's children's bookshelves as a quaint relic left over from a more innocent era. This child has a favorite pastime she calls the "Glad Game," in which she consistently looks upon the bright side of every adversity, and never accepts defeat. In the Pickford film, Pollyanna is the newly orphaned child of an Ozark missionary preacher who's sent for—out of "duty"—by her only living relative, a stern and embittered New England maiden aunt named Polly Harrington (Katherine Griffith). In this episodic narrative, Pollyanna repeatedly succeeds in displeasing Aunt Polly by always doing the

incorrect thing, getting into mischief and befriending a neighborhood orphan boy named Jimmy Bean (Howard Ralston).

The turning point comes when Pollyanna rescues a child from the path of an oncoming automobile and, in so doing, is herself struck down and crippled. Whereupon, Aunt Polly admits aloud, "I didn't realize how much she meant to me." And her niece expresses gladness that she *had* the accident, just because it made Aunt Polly, for the first time, actually call her "dear."

By the film's end, Pollyanna has not only defied the doctors who predicted she'd never walk again, but she has reunited the thawed-out Aunt Polly with a long-ago-rejected suitor and smoothed over the problems of everyone in her orbit in a whirlwind of Victorian Goodness and Gladness. At fadeout, we get a quick glimpse of a years-later Pollyanna and Jimmy Bean, apparently now wed; he's a streetcar conductor, and they're surrounded by a swarm of rambunctious little ones of their own.

Katherine Griffith, Mary Pickford and Howard Ralston.

Katherine Griffith and Mary Pickford

Mary Pickford may not personally have liked *Pollyanna*, but none of those negative feelings is evident on the screen. And it's through her charming performance, under the little-known Paul Powell's direction, that the movie still remains watchable, for all its "cuteness."

Pickford retired from acting at forty in 1933, following the failure of her sentimental drama *Secrets*. Her explanation was touching: "I left the screen because I didn't want what happened to Charlie Chaplin to happen to me. When he discarded the Little Tramp, the Little Tramp turned around and killed him. The Little Girl made me—I wasn't waiting for the Little Girl to kill me, too."

IF I WERE KING

1920

CREDITS

A Fox Film. Presented by William Fox. Directed by J. Gordon Edwards. Screenplay by E. Lloyd Sheldon. Based on the novel and stage play by Justin Huntly McCarthy. Eight reels.

CAST

William Farnum (*François Villon*); Betty Ross Clarke (*Katherine de Vaucelles*); Fritz Leiber (*Louis XI*); Walter Law (*Thibault*); Henry Carvill (*Triestan*); Claude Payton (*Montigney*); V. V. Clogg (*Toison D'Or*); Harold Clairmont (*Noel*); Renita Johnson (*Hugette*).

Justin McCarthy's durable 1901 novel *If I Were King*, about the exploits of the roguish 15th-century French poet François Villon, has enjoyed not a few incarnations in the theatrical media. McCarthy himself adapted his fiction to the stage, which version inspired the silent filmmakers. Selig Productions released a one-reel movie based on the work in 1911, and in 1920 it served as a vehicle for William Farnum, originally a stage actor like his equally popular brother Dustin.

McCarthy's play also inspired a 1927 John Barrymore movie, *The Beloved Rogue*, and reverted to its original title as a showcase for Ronald Colman in 1939. But probably it has received wider fame in its Rudolf Friml-William H. Post-Brian Hooker musical metamorphosis, as the operetta *The Vagabond King*, which was filmed twice, in 1930 and 1956.

William Farnum had been on the stage since he was nine, and was well into his thirties by the time he began acting for the early silent screen, achieving almost immediate success in the 1914 first film version of Rex Beach's *The Spoilers*, opposite Tom Santschi and Kathlyn Williams. *If I Were King*, was the ninth of twelve motion pictures Farnum starred in under J. Gordon Edwards, who had been the favorite director of that vamp of vamps, Theda Bara, Fox's biggest star of the late Teens. But when Bara left Fox and a waning career with which she had become dissatisfied, she also ended her fruitful professional alliance with Edwards.

William Farnum

Unidentified players, Fritz Leiber, William Farnum and Betsy Ross Clarke

Edwards then began his association with Farnum, whose rugged screen image, of course, represented quite the antithesis of Bara's. Together, Farnum and Edwards turned out a pair of Zane Grey Westerns, *The Last of the Duanes* (1919) and *The Lone Star Ranger* (1920), before turning to romantic costume dramas with 1920's *The Adventurer. If I Were King*, which followed, was probably their most successful collaboration of all, with Farnum assuming the adventurous Villon role that had already served E. H. Sothern so well on the stage.

Unfortunately, like most of the other films of Farnum and director Edwards, *If I Were King* has been lost to the ravages of time and the deterioration of celluloid. And so we are left with the evaluations of the critics of 1920, of which *Variety*'s negative opinion was in the minority. For, while predicting that a "hungry and undiscriminating" audience for such offerings would make this motion picture a hit, they regarded it as "misdirected, badly imagined and carried out in stilted fashion, with its best climaxes lost in the cutting room." Yet another trade publication, the super-critical *Harrison's Reports*, disagreed, calling *If I Were King* "an artistically produced costume play, with many light comedy situations and quite a few thrilling moments." And *The New York Times*, after reporting that the movie had already won the approval of its original author, called it "a spectacular, swiftly moving medieval melodrama," and singled out "that impossible, irresistible, extravagantly heroic person, François Villon, whom William Farnum brings to rosy life."

Then commanding a salary in the area of $10,000 a week, Farnum was among Hollywood's highest paid actors of 1920. Five years later, the actor suffered an injury while filming which thereafter relegated him to minor character parts, in which he continued until his death in 1953.

William Farnum, Betsy Ross Clarke and Fritz Leiber

WAY DOWN EAST

1920

Richard Barthelmess and Lillian Gish

Lillian Gish and Lowell Sherman

Lillian Gish.

CREDITS

A United Artists Picture. A D. W. Griffith Production. Produced and directed by D. W. Griffith. Associate Director: Elmer Clifton. Scenario by Anthony Paul Kelly and D. W. Griffith. Based on the stage play by Lottie Blair Parker, revised by Joseph R. Grismer. Photographed by G. W. "Billy" Bitzer and Hendrik Sartov. Edited by James Smith and Rose Smith. Art Direction by Charles O. Seessel and Clifford Pember. Technical Direction by Frank Wortman. Decorative Titles by Victor Georg. Production Assistant: Leigh Smith. Gowns by Lady Duff Gordon. Furs by Otto Kahn, Inc. Lillian Gish's gowns by O'Kane Cromwell. Music composed and selected by Louis Silvers and William F. Peters. Thirteen reels.

CAST

Lillian Gish (*Anna Moore*); Richard Barthelmess (*David Bartlett*); Lowell Sherman (*Lennox Sanderson*); Burr McIntosh (*Squire Bartlett*); Kate Bruce (*Mrs. Bartlett*); Vivia Ogden (*Martha Perkins*); Creighton Hale (*Professor Sterling*); Mary Hay (*Kate Brewster*); Porter Strong (*Seth Holcomb*); Edgar Nelson (*Hi Holler*); Emily Fitzroy (*Maria Poole*); George Neville (*Constable Reuben Whipple*); Mrs. David Landau (*Anna Moore's Mother*); Josephine Bernard (*Mrs. Tremont*); Mrs. Morgan Belmont (*Diana Tremont*); Patricia Fruen (*Her Sister*); Norma Shearer (*Extra in barn-dance sequence*); residents of White River Junction, Vermont (*Extras*).

Lottie Blair Parker's 1898 stage melodrama *Way Down East* had for years been one of the most popular plays in the U.S. when producer-director D. W. Griffith elected to bring it to the silent screen. Immediately, he drew criticism and ridicule from his industry peers by paying $175,000 for the rights—more than the entire cost of his 1915 classic *The Birth of a Nation*. As Lillian Gish recalls in her 1969 memoir *The Movies, Mr. Griffith and Me*, "We all thought privately that Mr. Griffith had lost his mind. *Way Down East* was a horse-and-buggy melodrama, familiar on the rural circuit for more than twenty years. We didn't believe it would ever succeed."

Griffith sorely needed a successful picture at that time, and a dedicated cast and crew combined forces to make even the more sophisticated audiences of 1920 accept *Way Down East*'s excesses involving Anna (Gish), an innocent country girl duped by a city playboy (Lowell

D.W. Griffith directing Vivia Ogden, Richard Barthelmess, Lillian Gish, Burr McIntosh and Lowell Sherman

Burr McIntosh, Kate Bruce, Lowell Sherman, Lillian Gish, Vivia Ogden (partially hidden), Mary Hay, Creighton Hale, George Neville, Richard Barthelmess and Edgar Nelson

Richard Barthelmess and Lillian Gish

Sherman) into a phony marriage that falls apart when she becomes pregnant. Abandoned by her "husband," Anna gives birth, but her baby dies as it's being baptized. The young woman then finds employment on a farm, where her new life is threatened by an awkward coincidence: her betrayer happens to own the farm next door and, when he discovers her living there, unsuccessfully attempts to force her departure. Eventually, Anna's secret past is revealed and she's literally ordered out of the farmhouse into a raging blizzard. Blinded by the snow, she wanders onto an icy river, where she's ultimately saved from going over a waterfall by the farmer's nimblefooted son David (an almost unbelievably beautiful young Richard Barthelmess), whose love she had previously rejected, because of her past. A climactic wedding assures the film's audience of Anna's rosy future with David.

With the interior and farm scenes filmed in Griffith's New York studios at Mamaroneck, the director sought greater realism for his exteriors by taking his company in late winter to White River Junction, Vermont, where he filmed scenes on and around the icy river, and where, reported Lillian Gish, "The temperature never rose above zero during the three weeks we worked there." For Gish, this location was especially rugged, since she spent most of those scenes attired only in a woolen dress, either running or lying in a faint on a slab of ice. This had to be dynamited to create the effect of a perilous ice floe moving down-river and over a high waterfall, for which shots of Niagara were used. Clever editing matched these location scenes with others shot later with wooden ice-cakes at Farmington, Connecticut. Back in Mamaroneck, a fortuitous blizzard enabled Griffith to photograph most of the storm sequence right outside his studios there.

Describing the hardships of shooting *Way Down East*, Lillian Gish further remembers, "This kind of dedication probably seems foolish today, but it wasn't unusual then.

No sacrifice was too great to get the film right, to get it accurate, true and perfect. We weren't important in our minds; only the picture was. Mr. Griffith felt the same way."

For most of the intervening sixty-odd years, *Way Down East* has been available to the public only in a much-truncated form, due largely to Griffith's own long-ago efforts to "improve" his movie by editing it for length and to reduce the broadly played "comic relief," involving subsidiary characters little seen in the film's shortened versions. And so it came as quite a revelation to many when, in June of 1984, New York's Museum of Modern Art offered two showings of a lengthy restored print, the result of a laborious five-year project aided by the contributions of private collectors and the discovery, in the Library of Congress, of Griffith's own shot-by-shot analysis of *Way Down East*'s original continuity.

Having seen both long and short versions of Griffith's classic melodrama, one is left with indelible memories of that fantastic rescue-from-the-ice-floe climax and, above all, with the strikingly affecting acting of Lillian Gish. Griffith cunningly reveals her in telling close-up during each of her Big Moments: the revelation that her marriage isn't valid; her silent scream upon discovering that her newly-baptized infant has died; and the spirited accusation against her smug seducer, delivered just minutes before she's driven out into the storm by her self-righteous employer. Here Gish's warmly expressive face reveals a truth and inner light that continues to illuminate that unique talent generations after it was captured so beautifully by the cameras of Griffith's reliable Billy Bitzer and his assistant Hendrik Sartov.

Creaky though *Way Down East* may look to filmgoers of the Eighties, this audience-pleaser of 1920-21 still remains effective, especially in the timeless performance of that strong but vulnerable lady, Lillian Gish.

THE MARK OF ZORRO

1920

CREDITS

A United Artists Picture. A Douglas Fairbanks Pictures Corp. Production. Directed by Fred Niblo. Screenplay by Elton Thomas (Douglas Fairbanks). Based on Johnston McCulley's *All-Story Weekly* magazine serial *The Curse of Capistrano*. Photographed by William McGann and Harry Thorpe. Art Direction by Edward Langley. Seven reels.

CAST

Douglas Fairbanks (*Don Diego Vega/Señor Zorro*); Noah Beery (*Sgt. Pedro Gonzales*); Marguerite de la Motte (*Lolita*); Charles Hill Mailes (*Don Carlos Pulido*); Robert McKim (*Capt. Juan Ramon*); Claire McDowell (*Doña Catalina*); George Periolat (*Governor Alvarado*); Walt Whitman (*Fray Felipe*); Sidney de Grey (*Don Alejandro Pulido*); Tote du Crow (*Bernardo*).

Throughout the Teens, stage-trained Douglas Fairbanks had romped through a succession of popular comedy-dramas displaying athletic ability, a cheerful, dauntless personality and an all-American-boy appeal in movies like *His Picture in the Papers* (1916), *Flirting with Fate* (1916), *His Majesty the American* (1919) and *A Modern Musketeer* (1918). But in *The Mark of Zorro*, his thirtieth feature film, the actor risked his popularity by switching to swashbuckling adventure, and successfully launched the series of costume movies for which he's now best remembered, especially *The Three Musketeers* (1921), *Robin Hood* (1922) and *The Thief of Bagdad* (1924).

The character of Zorro originated in *All-Story Weekly* magazine in 1919 with Johnston McCulley's five-part serial *The Curse of Capistrano*, which concerned itself with a dashing, masked Robin Hood fighting against political corruption in Old California. Fairbanks purchased rights to the character and, under the pseudonym "Elton Thomas," adapted the story into a screen scenario he called *The Mark of Zorro* (in 1925, he also turned out

Douglas Fairbanks and Marguerite de la Motte

Douglas Fairbanks

a somewhat less effective sequel, *Don Q, Son of Zorro*).

The dual-role of foppish Don Diego Vega and his dashing alter-ego, the mysterious Señor Zorro, owes something to the Scarlet Pimpernel, and anticipates such popular later folk-heroes as Superman, Batman, and the Red Shadow of Romberg's operetta *The Desert Song*. For each of those is a disarmingly ineffectual (if not downright unmasculine) individual who doubles as an aggressive do-gooder battling for the rights of his less-motivated neighbors.

The Mark of Zorro is set in 1820's California, where the foppish nobleman Don Diego Vega (Fairbanks) enjoys a double life, masquerading in a black outfit with mask, gun and sword to correct local injustice. His father directs Diego to court the beautiful Lolita (Marguerite de la Motte), but he's unable to make any inroads in her affections—except when he reappears as the exciting Señor Zorro. When the young lady and her family are imprisoned as traitors by the corrupt Governor Alvarado (George Periolat) and his flunky Captain Ramon (Robert McKim), Zorro organizes California's aristocratic caballeros to join him in defeating this administration. At the finale, Zorro/Don Diego unmasks for Lolita, and there is obviously a wedding in their future.

Fairbanks need not have worried about this alteration in his screen image. Although a Beverly Hills sneak-preview generated little enthusiasm (prompting the star to return immediately to his old milieu with *The Nut*, a 1921 failure), *Zorro*'s release brought an entirely different reaction—and the biggest hit of Fairbanks' career. For the remainder of the decade, "colorful," "romantic" and "swashbuckling" would be the words synonymous with the Fairbanks name.

Aside from such fringe-movie uses of the Zorro character as three Republic serials, a Walt Disney television series and a Seventies porno-spoof, the years have brought us a 1940 remake of *The Mark of Zorro* with Tyrone Power, a 1974 TV-movie starring Frank Langella, that same year's European-made counterpart with Alain Delon and, most recently, George Hamilton's 1981 farcical "last word" on the famous dual-character, *Zorro, the Gay Blade*.

Douglas Fairbanks, Marguerite de la Motte and Robert McKim

Lon Chaney

Priscilla Dean,
Wheeler Oakman and
Lon Chaney

OUTSIDE THE LAW

1921

CREDITS

A Universal-Jewel Picture. Presented by Carl Laemmle. Directed by Tod Browning. Scenario by Tod Browning and Lucien Hubbard. Titles by Gardner Bradford. Photographed by William Fildew. Art Direction by E. E. Sheeley. Eight reels.

CAST

Priscilla Dean (*Molly "Silky Moll" Madden*); Wheeler Oakman (*"Dapper Bill" Ballard*); Lon Chaney (*"Black Mike" Sylva/Ah Wing*); Ralph Lewis (*"Silent" Madden*); E. A. Warren (*Chang Lo*); Stanley Goethals (*"That Kid"*); Melbourne MacDowell (*Morgan Spencer*); Wilton Taylor (*Inspector*).

Priscilla Dean, Lon Chaney and Wheeler Oakman

Priscilla Dean was twenty-five and at the height of her career in 1921 when she starred (hers was the solo name over the film's title) in *Outside the Law*, a particularly well-made crook melodrama. Like most of her best films as queen of the Universal lot, this one was directed by that master of sinister themes, Tod Browning, her successful collaborator on *The Wicked Darling* (1919), *The Exquisite Thief* (1919) and *The Virgin of Stamboul* (1920). Dean must also have felt secure in re-teaming, in *Outside the Law*, with her offscreen husband Wheeler Oakman and character actor Lon Chaney, with whom she played in a pair of 1919 melodramas, *The Wicked Darling* and *Paid in Advance*.

At thirty-four, Chaney, with an impressive and lengthy array of movie credits behind him, was then on the brink of graduating to full-fledged stardom at Universal, which would happen two years later with his masterful delineation of *The Hunchback of Notre Dame*. But in *Outside the Law*, he's still very much a featured player, albeit a skilled and versatile one, as evidenced by the ease with which he handles *two* roles, that of the crafty gangster "Black Mike" and the Chinese servant Ah Wing who, in the final reel, shoots down the gang boss. Which means that Chaney, through the magic of double-exposure, literally kills *himself* on screen!

Set in San Francisco's Chinatown, this contemporary crime yarn introduces Priscilla Dean as an experienced "society thief" who, along with her crooked father (Ralph Lewis), is on the verge of going straight. But those ideas are cast aside when Lewis is framed by Chaney and sent to jail. The latter then plots vengeance on Dean (whom he hates, for some unexplained reason) by conniving with henchman Wheeler Oakman to involve her in a jewel robbery, for which Dean alone will be blamed. But Oakman falls for the girl and betrays Chaney's plot. This leads to a long sojourn during which the couple hide out in an apartment house. Eventually, however, they decide to give up the gems, return them and reform by marrying and leading an ordinary family life. But Chaney discovers their whereabouts and confronts them, leading to a Chinatown shoot-out during which Chinese Chaney rubs out Caucasian Chaney.

Priscilla Dean is scarcely remembered today, and few of her movies appear to have survived. Fortunately, a print of *Outside the Law* was discovered a few years ago in Wisconsin, and has been restored so that present and future generations can rediscover, through her expressive performance, that early silent-film acting wasn't necessarily all wild gestures and overexaggeration, even in melodrama.

Claire Windsor and Louis Calhern

TOO WISE WIVES

1921

CREDITS

A Paramount Picture. A Famous Players-Lasky Production. Produced, directed and written by Lois Weber. From a Story by Lois Weber and Marion Orth. Photographed by William C. Foster. Six reels.

CAST

Louis Calhern (*David Graham*); Claire Windsor (*Marie Graham*); Phillips Smalley (*John Daly*); Mona Lisa (*Sara Daly*).

In the early silent era, when America's film industry was ruled by men, one woman filmmaker—Lois Weber—made a valuable contribution to the screen by exploring bold social themes in movies which she not only produced and directed but also wrote, often with the aid of her husband, actor Phillips Smalley.

Born in 1882, Weber had begun as a concert pianist and musical-comedy actress, entering motion pictures in 1911 as a performer, usually co-starred with her spouse. A year later, she directed her first film, *The Troubadour's Triumph*. Thereafter, often in partnership with Smalley, Lois Weber continued to direct their movies as well as write and star in them, commanding the highest salary of any woman in the industry. In 1916, she formed Lois Weber Productions, that year turning out a controversial motion picture called *Where Are My Children?* that had the courage to advocate birth control as well as deal with abortion. It was reportedly shot at a cost of $12,000 and earned over $500,000. By 1920, Weber had turned out at least seventy-five movies, including many one- and two-reel shorts. Few dealt with frivolous subject matter; topics like adultery, prostitution and contemporary women's issues concerned her most. As a result, Lois Weber films gained a large female following, with titles like *The Price of a Good Time* (1917), *When a Girl Loves* (1919) and *To Please One Woman* (1920).

Too Wise Wives, one of four 1921 releases produced and directed by Weber, contrasted the lives of two married women, one a wife who tries too hard to please her husband, and by so doing nearly loses him to a married "other woman." But the restless husband rejects this would-be temptress, who then returns to her *own* husband, leaving the film's central couple to reconcile. Like most of Lois Weber's movies, *Too Wise Wives* was well-produced and obviously pitched to the distaff audience.

As David and Marie Graham, Weber cast Louis Calhern and one of her prettiest "discoveries," Claire Windsor. Both were then in their early twenties, and continued to star in several other Weber films before moving on to other studios.

As for Lois Weber, her vogue soon appeared to decline. And when she again attempted sensitive themes with *Sensation Seekers* (1926) and *The Angel of Broadway* (1927), the major distributors refused to handle them, much as they also sidestepped her final effort, *White Heat*, a forgotten 1934 melodrama mixing interracial love with marital infidelity. By that time, Dorothy Arzner had replaced Weber as Hollywood's foremost woman director.

Claire Windsor and Louis Calhern

Lois Wilson and Milton Sills

MISS LULU BETT

1921

CREDITS

A Paramount Picture. A Famous Players-Lasky Production. Presented by Adolph Zukor. Directed by William C. de Mille. Scenario by Clara Beranger. Based on the novel and play by Zona Gale. Photographed by L. Guy Wilky. Seven reels.

CAST

Lois Wilson (*Lulu Bett*); Milton Sills (*Neil Cornish*); Theodore Roberts (*Dwight Deacon*); Helen Ferguson (*Diana Deacon*); Mabel Van Buren (*Mrs. Dwight Deacon*); May Giraci (*Manona Deacon*); Clarence Burton (*Ninian Deacon*); Ethel Wales (*Grandma Bett*); Taylor Graves (*Bobby Larkin*); Charles Ogle (*Station Agent*).

Cecil B. DeMille, that flamboyant showman of the movie spectacle and the quasi-religious drama remains a director of legend in film history. But his older brother William (who, significantly, employed a more modest small "de" in his name), father of the celebrated dancer-choreographer Agnes de Mille, was the director who had a more profound—if quieter—effect on the silent screen.

William de Mille's films are less widely known today than Cecil's, and, unfortunately, most of them have now disappeared. Among the survivors, however, is one of his best, *Miss Lulu Bett*. This adaptation of Zona Gale's popular 1920 novel and Pulitzer Prize-winning drama adheres more closely to the book than the play, whose ending was altered in the interests of stage license. The movie also represented an ideal collaboration of director and star, for Lois Wilson, contemporary sources concurred, could hardly have submerged herself more completely in the title character had it been her own personal story. Decades later, asked about her favorite picture, a long-retired Wilson—with a salute to 1923's more renowned *The Covered Wagon*—nevertheless named *Miss Lulu Bett* as her choice, explaining, "It was a character part and I loved every moment of it. Mr. William de Mille was a great director."

Following on the heels of the Women's Suffrage Movement, *Miss Lulu Bett* tells of a plain young spinster who works for her married sister's family as a household drudge in a small town of the Twenties. Leaving this servitude to marry her brother-in-law's brother (Clarence Burton), Lulu discovers that he's already wed to another. Defying local gossip, she walks out on this "marriage" to lead an independent life with a job in the town bakery, where she's courted by a more suitable beau, the village schoolteacher (Milton Sills), whom she eventually weds.

Lois Wilson's performance never fails to reflect truth, or move her audience, as she grows from the self-effacing domestic to full realization of independence as a woman of character and beauty. But de Mille's subtle direction keeps the movie's characters as believable as his American small-town milieu is recognizable. His attention to everyday detail is meticulous, and his observation of human foibles uncanny. *Miss Lulu Bett* represents a quiet milestone of naturalistic quality in the films of the early Twenties.

Milton Sills and Lois Wilson

Clarence Burton and Lois Wilson

ORPHANS OF THE STORM

1921

CREDITS

A United Artists Picture. A D. W. Griffith Production. Produced and directed by D. W. Griffith. Scenario by Marquis de Trolignac (D. W. Griffith); based on the play *The Two Orphans* by Adolphe Philippe D'Ennery and Eugene Cormon, and its English adaptation by N. Hart Jackson and Albert Marshman. Photographed by Hendrik Sartov, Paul Allen and G. W. Bitzer. Art Direction by Charles M. Kirk. Set Designs by Edward Scholl. Technical Director: Frank Wortman. Music arranged by Louis F. Gottschalk and William Frederick Peters. Fourteen reels.

CAST

Lillian Gish (*Henriette Girard*); Dorothy Gish (*Louise*); Joseph Schildkraut (*The Chevalier de Vaudry*); Frank Losee (*The Count de Linieres*); Katherine Emmett (*The Countess de Linieres*); Lucille La Verne (*Mother Frochard*); Morgan Wallace (*The Marquis de Praille*); Sheldon Lewis (*Jacques Frochard*); Frank Puglia (*Pierre Frochard*); Creighton Hale (*Picard*); Leslie King (*Jacques-Forget-Not*); Monte Blue (*Danton*); Sidney Herbert (*Robespierre*); Lee Kohlmar (*King Louis XVI*); Adolphe Lestina (*Doctor*); Kate Bruce (*Sister Geneviève*); Flora Finch (*Starving Peasant*); Louis Wolheim (*Executioner*); Kenny Delmar (*The Chevalier, as a Boy*); Herbert Sutch (*Meat-Carver at Fête*); James Smith and Rose Smith (*Dancers*).

Lillian Gish has reported that this film was made in place of *Faust*, which D. W. Griffith had his mind set on filming, but which she knew would never have been a money-maker, and consequently set about persuading him otherwise, in the wake of his unsuccessful *Dream Street* (1921). Originally, *Orphans of the Storm* began shooting under the title of the long-popular but even-then creaky old stage melodrama on which it was loosely based, *The Two Orphans*. Unfortunately, an Italian movie of the same story and title beat Griffith's motion picture into American release; another then-current version from Germany remained in the Griffith vaults for safe-keeping. But to avoid any further confusion, Griffith's *The Two Orphans* became *Orphans of the Storm* just prior to its late-December Boston release in 1921.

Actually, that stage melodrama had nothing whatsoever to do with the French Revolution. That was all Griffith's doing, designed to add sweep, spectacle and color to this rather Dickensian story about the misadventures of two young girls, one of whom is blind. And, as noted by most critics and historians, *Orphans of the Storm* also owes a great deal of its effectiveness to Griffith's generous borrowings from *A Tale of Two Cities* in its details and reflections. These include the accidental killing of a poor child by an unfeeling aristocrat's carriage and, of course, the Bastille's storming by the impoverished and hungry Parisian masses. But Griffith also drew upon Thomas Carlyle's 1837 account, *The History of the French Revolution*, with meticulous attention to historical accuracy of the period.

It has been said that, with this production, Griffith wanted to outdo Ernst Lubitsch's French Revolution spectacle *Madame Dubarry* (1919), and so he set about constructing fourteen acres of sets representing eighteenth-century Paris at his New York State studios on Mamaroneck's Orienta Point. His stars, Lillian and Dorothy Gish, siblings of no career rivalry whatsoever (Lillian excelled in drama, while Dorothy's forte was light comedy), had both started out in movies under Griffith's direction in *The Unseen Enemy* (1912). *Orphans of the Storm* and *Romola* (1924) marked their only teamings during the Twenties. And, despite their off-screen closeness, the sisters would not professionally reunite until 1956 and a summer theatre tour of Enid Bagnold's *The Chalk Garden*.

Orphans of the Storm casts Dorothy as Louise, an illegitimate child of the wealthy de Vaudrey family, who abandon her on the steps of a church. From there, she's adopted by a worker named Girard, who brings her up along with his own natural daughter Henriette (played by Lillian). But a plague kills the elder Girards, at the same time blinding the unfortunate Louise. Henriette vows never to marry or leave her adopted sister's side until she regains her sight.

En route to Paris, the girls are threatened by the nefarious Marquis de Praille (Morgan Wallace), who has designs on Henriette. Upon their arrival, she is kidnapped by the Marquis, while Louise is taken under the enterprising wing of a conniving beggar woman, Mother Frochard (acted to the hilt by the shamelessly hammy Lucille La Verne). Griffith now juxtaposes the two separated girls' stories with that of the rise of the Revolutionaries. The stirring melodrama reaches a thrilling, well-edited climax with an about-to-be-guillotined Henriette rescued at the eleventh hour through the desperate efforts of Danton

Frank Puglia, Lucille La-
Verne, Sheldon Lewis, Dorothy Gish.

Lillian and Dorothy Gish

Dorothy and Lillian Gish

(Monte Blue), in time for a reunion with her well-born lover (Joseph Schildkraut in his handsome, pre-character days) and the no-longer-blind Louise.

Orphans of the Storm is still a rewarding movie, reflecting the care and cost obviously lavished upon its production. Both Gish sisters reflect everything their dramatic roles call for, and they're excellently supported by a huge and effective cast, including the amusingly sinister Robespierre of Sidney Herbert, described in a title as "the original pussy-footer," and indeed looking like a powdered-wigged Pink Panther.

Deservedly, *Orphans of the Storm* proved a great success and a major attraction during its general release in 1922. But, due to heavy exploitation and road-show losses, Griffith's last great film spectacle did not earn as much as it deserved to. For the Gishes, this was their final professional alliance with their mentor, D. W. Griffith. Lillian has recalled that the great director, perhaps anticipating the actress's interest in choosing her own scripts and directors, advised her: "You should go out on your own. Your name is of as much value as mine with the public, and I think in your own interest you ought to capitalize on it while you can." Consequently, she left for Italy and *The White Sister*, while Dorothy joined the Havana-based cast of *The Bright Shawl*.

Louis Wolheim (atop platform), Monte Blue, Joseph Schildkraut, Lillian and Dorothy Gish

Rudolph Valentino

MORAN OF THE LADY LETTY

1922

CREDITS

A Paramount Picture. Presented by Jesse L. Lasky. Directed by George Melford. Screenplay by Monte M. Katterjohn. Based on the novel by Frank Norris. Photographed by William Marshall. Seven reels.

CAST

Dorothy Dalton (*Letty Sternersen/aka "Moran"*); Rudolph Valentino (*Ramon Laredo*); Charles Brinley (*Capt. Sternersen*); Walter Long (*Capt. "Frisco" Kitchell*); Emil Jorgenson (*Nels*); Maude Wayne (*Josephine Herrick*); Cecil Holland (*Bill Trim*); George Kuwa (*"Chopstick" Charlie*); Charles K. French (*Tavern Owner*); George O'Brien (*Deck Hand*); William Boyd (*Extra*).

Although her name will mean little or nothing to today's movie buffs, in the late Teens and early Twenties Dorothy Dalton was a big favorite. She had studied at the American Conservatory of Dramatic Art, gaining practical experience in vaudeville on the Orpheum Circuit, as well as with stock companies. During a Los Angeles engagement, she atttracted the attention of movie mogul Thomas H. Ince, who signed her to a personal contract, directing a number of her films himself. From the Ince Company, she later moved over to Paramount, but gave up a successful career at thirty to marry Oscar Hammerstein's Broadway producer son Arthur in 1924.

A glance at Dorothy Dalton's filmography reveals only a collection of long forgotten titles of the "romantic melodrama" variety, such as *The Flame of the Yukon* (1917), *The Kaiser's Shadow* (1918), *Market of Souls* (1919) and *Guilty of Love* (1920). The sole exception, 1922's *Moran*

Dorothy Dalton, Rudolph Valentino, Emil Jorgenson and George Kuwa.

of the Lady Letty, undoubtedly owes its modest degree of historical interest to the young actor who played opposite her—Rudolph Valentino. For Valentino, this rugged saltwater adventure yarn marked an important change of pace. After too many roles of the "lounge lizard" or elegant-romantic-hero variety, *Moran of the Lady Letty* offered the actor an opportunity to prove his manliness in a part that could appeal to men as well as the women who already flocked in droves to his films.

Shot largely on location in and about the San Francisco waterfront, *Moran of the Lady Letty* cast Valentino as Ramon Laredo, a socialite who is shanghaied aboard a pirate ship plying its trade in the waters between coastal California and Western Mexico. They encounter the *Lady Letty*, whose burning coal cargo has asphyxiated all but the skipper's somewhat masculine-looking daughter Letty, who goes by the name of "Moran." The pirates rescue her, and Ramon is attracted to the young captive. In Mexico, her rescuers plan to sell Moran as a slave to an outlaw. But Ramon organizes the crew, and a battle ensues between them and the outlaw's men.

The plot grows considerably thicker before its exciting climax, a knock-down, drag-out fight between Ramon and the ship's evil Captain Kitchell (Walter Long)—a battle that ranges from the ship's cabin up into the rigging, whence the villain falls sixty feet to his death.

For Valentino, this two-fisted role proved a revelation. As Ramon, he was not only believable as the clean-cut youth who learns about hard work and the battle for survival, but his film image became both more masculine and natural. Curiously enough, *Moran of the Lady Letty* was not liked by either Valentino or his wife, Natacha Rambova. The star held certain illusions about his screen image, and felt that so naturalistic a story as this could only lessen his attraction as a romantic movie idol.

Alla Nazimova and Alan Hale

A DOLL'S HOUSE

1922

CREDITS

A United Artists Picture. A Nazimova Production. Directed by Charles Bryant. Scenario by Peter M. Winters (aka Alla Nazimova). Based on the play by Henrik Ibsen. Photographed by Charles Van Enger. Seven reels.

CAST

Alan Hale (*Torvald Helmer*); Alla Nazimova (*Nora Helmer*); Nigel de Brulier (*Dr. Rank*); Elinor Oliver (*Anna*); Wedgwood Nowell (*Nils Krogstad*); Cara Lee (*Ellen*); Florence Fisher (*Mrs. Linden*); Philippe de Lacy (*Ivar*); Barbara Maier (*Emmy*).

Russian-born Alla Nazimova—an actress best known merely by her last name—has become a dim and shadowy figure in the legendary annals of stage and screen history. Some sources indicate that she was a notorious lesbian whose Hollywood "sewing circle" included as her protégée Rudolph Valentino's exotic second wife, the talented designer-actress who went by the name Natacha Rambova. Others point to her devoted common-law marriage to director Charles Bryant, who long passed for her legal husband—until his departure to wed another drove Nazimova to the brink of suicide.

But whatever the truth about the actress's personal life, she established a distinguished reputation on the stage, especially for her interpretations of the great Ibsen heroines of *The Master Builder*, *Hedda Gabler* and *A Doll's House*. Of this trio, the latter two remain perhaps the most difficult to portray successfully. But the 1879 *A Doll's House* has proven the most challenging to film actresses, five of whom have tackled it to date: Dorothy Phillips and Elsie Ferguson, in respective silent adaptations of 1917 and 1918; Nazimova four years later; and, after a passage of fifty-one years—amid an era of feminist consciousness-raising—two separate 1973 versions headlining Claire Bloom and Jane Fonda.

In its third silent incarnation, Nazimova's 1922 offering marked the first movie financed with her own money for United Artists release and employing her own adaptation,

Alan Hale and Alla Nazimova

Alla Nazimova and Florence Fisher

written under the pseudonym of "Peter M. Winters." Charles Bryant directed this rather stagebound drama about Nora Helmer, the wife who commits forgery to save her husband's health, only to be faced, years later, with the threat of blackmail—a situation that reveals the true nature of her overbearing mate, thus motivating Nora to walk out on both him and her children.

Nazimova's performance, ably supported by Alan Hale as Torvald Helmer, the male chauvinistic husband, was both praised and criticized, and it's not difficult to understand why. An actress in the grand manner, Nazimova was at her best on the *stage*, where her powerful style carried easily to the most distant seat. Scaling this technique down to meet the requirements of the motion picture sometimes eluded her, and in *A Doll's House*, some of her most dramatic moments are too big for the intimate medium, where each glance and gesture are so greatly magnified. Occasionally, her acting is overly mannered, yet this film represents a laudable effort to bring Ibsen to the screen. Its failure at the box-office could not deter Nazimova from what would become her costliest screen folly—the outrageously bizarre 1923 *Salome*, which aimed at serious movie art and yielded only "camp" at its loftiest.

Alla Nazimova

BEAUTY'S WORTH

1922

Marion Davies (center)

CREDITS

A Paramount Picture. A Cosmopolitan Production. Directed by Robert G. Vignola. Screenplay by Luther Reed. Based on the *Saturday Evening Post* story by Sophie Kerr. Photographed by Ira H. Morgan. Sets by Joseph Urban. Seven reels.

CAST

Marion Davies (*Prudence Cole*); Forrest Stanley (*Cheyne Rovein*); June Elvidge (*Amy Tillson*); Truly Shattuck (*Mrs. Garrison*); Lydia Yeamans Titus (*Jane*); Hallam Cooley (*Henry Garrison*); Antrim Short (*Tommy*); Thomas Jefferson (*Peter*); Martha Mattox (*Aunt Elizabeth Whitney*); Aileen Manning (*Aunt Cynthia Whitney*); John Dooley (*Soldier in Charade Scene*); Gordon Dooley (*Doll in Charade Scene*).

Over the years, actress Marion Davies—the Follies girl with whom publishing tycoon William Randolph Hearst fell in love and fruitlessly tried to make Hollywood's biggest star—has been much maligned for a lack of dramatic talent, accorded belated praise for her comedy roles of the late Twenties, and ridiculed in the thinly disguised portrayal of "Susan Alexander" in the 1941 Orson Welles masterpiece *Citizen Kane*.

It was a fate this sweet, pretty, fun-loving and good-natured young woman hardly deserved, even though her uneven, twenty-year movie career (1917–1937) owed everything to the Hearst millions. He established the production company that turned out her films, and spared no expense in providing Davies with the industry's best craftsmen and popular co-stars. Everything was done to make Marion look good. Unfortunately, that "look" had to correspond with W. R.'s idealized vision of her—in costume romances, or as a virginal heroine sought for her beauty.

When they first met, the showgirl was only nineteen and the publisher, a married man with children, in his mid-fifties. Yet their subsequent alliance endured until Hearst's death in 1951, fourteen years after both he and his mistress had quietly closed the door on her ebbing film career.

Beauty's Worth was the first of five Hearst-sponsored Cosmopolitan films to star Marion Davies in 1922. It was little more than a routine Cinderella story about a plain Quaker girl who flourishes under the influence of a sympathetic artist (played by Forrest Stanley) as she

attempts to please a snobbish socialite (Hallam Cooley), whom she thinks she loves. Of course, at the film's close, it's the artist who wins the Quaker maid.

Beauty's Worth has its moments, particularly those scenes in which Davies blossoms forth as the main attraction in an elaborate series of charade pantomimes (staged for the amusement of society guests at a seaside resort hotel). But her acting limitations were obvious enough to draw harsh criticism from *The New York Times*, whose reviewer appeared to resent the money evidently lavished on the film's production. In 1922, Marion Davies remained little more than a beautiful young movie star whose career mismanagement was beyond her control. Five years later, her celluloid future would be brighter, highlighted by her unexpected skill in a pair of 1928 films directed by King Vidor, *The Patsy* and *Show People*.

Antrim Short, Marion Davies, June Elvidge and unidentified player.

OLIVER TWIST

1922

CREDITS

As Associated First National Picture. A Jackie Coogan Production. Produced by Sol Lesser. Directed by Frank Lloyd. Screenplay by Frank Lloyd and Harry Weil. Based on the novel by Charles Dickens. Titles by Walter Anthony. Photographed by Glen MacWilliams and Robert Martin. Edited by Irene Morra. Lighting effects by Louis Johnson. Art Direction by Stephen Goosson. Costumes by Walter J. Israel. Eight reels.

CAST

Jackie Coogan (*Oliver Twist*); Lon Chaney (*Fagin*); Gladys Brockwell (*Nancy Sikes*); George Siegmann (*Bill Sikes*); Lionel Belmore (*Mr. Brownlow*); James Marcus (*Mr. Bumble*); Aggie Herring (*The Widow Corney*); Edouard Trebaol (*Jack Dawkins, "The Artful Dodger"*); Taylor Graves (*Charlie Bates*); Carl Stockdale (*Monks*); Lewis Sargent (*Noah Claypool*); Joan Standing (*Charlotte*); Joseph H. Hazleton (*Mr. Grimwig*); Nelson McDowell (*Mr. Sowerberry*); Esther Ralston (*Rose Maylie*); Florence Hale (*Mrs. Bedwin*); Eddie Roland (*Toby Crackitt*); Gertrude Claire (*Mrs. Maylie*).

Jackie Coogan

Charles Dickens's densely plotted classic, first published serially over the years 1837–39, runs a close second to his *A Christmas Carol* in its popularity with filmmakers over the years, having reached the screen at least ten times since 1909. This seventh movie of that tale of an orphaned boy's misadventures among the low-life thieves and child-exploiters of early 19th-century London was turned out with evident care taken in its sets, costumes and atmospheric lighting. And the adaptation of as much of the book as it encompasses is quite reasonably faithful to the source material, while simplifying and omitting some of the more nebulous Dickensian detail.

At seven, Jackie Coogan was by then a box-office child star of considerable draw, and this film affords him sufficient opportunities to demonstrate the adorable charm and acting talent that brought him almost "overnight" fame with Charlie Chaplin in 1921's *The Kid*. But it seems a bit odd that, in this *Oliver Twist*—indeed, a

Jackie Coogan Productions effort, supervised by Coogan, Sr.—the little tyke is quite frequently *off the screen*, while the script focuses on the various other characters that populate its milieu. Thus, director Frank Lloyd's cameras spend a good deal of time on the plot twists involving Fagin, Bill Sikes, Nancy and Monks, well portrayed by the respective talents of Lon Chaney, George Siegmann, Gladys Brockwell and Carl Stockdale. Fagin, in fact, has seldom been played with less adherence to racial stereotyping, and Chaney (of whom young Coogan had no kind memories) won considerable praise for his work here, characteristically disguised by heavy make-up and stooped, crablike movements. A year later, this seasoned and popular character actor would finally graduate into the top ranks with his striking performance in *The Hunchback of Notre Dame*.

The film's director and co-author, Frank Lloyd, was a Scotsman who had originally been an actor who graduated to directing after having his fill of playing heavies in a succession of Universal Westerns. In 1917, he had previously tackled Dickens with his direction of the second screen version of *A Tale of Two Cities*, a vehicle for William Farnum. The 1920 adaptation of *Madame X*, starring Pauline Frederick, brought him further attention, and the press had nothing but good things to say about his handling of the Coogan *Oliver Twist*. Lloyd went on to win a pair of Academy Awards in the late-silent/early-talkie period for his direction of 1929's *The Divine Lady* and 1933's *Cavalcade*.

Lon Chaney, Jackie Coogan, Taylor Graves, George Siegmann and Gladys Brockwell

DOWN TO THE SEA IN SHIPS

1922

CREDITS

W. W. Hodkinson release of a Whaling Film Corp. Production. Produced and directed by Elmer Clifton. Story and scenario by John L. E. Pell. Photographed by Alexander G. Penrod. Additional photography by Paul Allen, Maurice E. Kains and Albert Doubrava. Music score by Henry F. Gilbert. Twelve reels.

CAST

Marguerite Courtot (*Patience Morgan*); Raymond McKee (*Thomas Allen Dexter*); J. Thornton Baston (*Samuel Siggs*); William Walcott (*Charles W. Morgan*); Clara Bow (*"Dot" Morgan*); James Turfler (*Jimmie*); William Cavanaugh (*Henry Morgan*); Leigh R. Smith (*"Scuff" Smith*); Elizabeth Foley (*Baby Patience Morgan*); Thomas White (*Baby Tommy Dexter*); Juliette Courtot (*"Judy" Peggs*); Clarice Vance (*Nahoma*); Ada Laycock (*"Henny" Clark*); Pat Hartigan (*Jake Finner*); Curtis Pierce (*Town Crier*); Capt. James A. Tilton (*Captain of the* Morgan).

In 1949, 20th Century-Fox released a fine whaling drama by this title with Richard Widmark, Dean Stockwell and Lionel Barrymore—but there the similarity to this 1922 movie ends, for their storylines bear no resemblance whatsoever. However, it's interesting to note that, while the later film confined its exterior scenes to studio sets and its whaling action to technical ingenuity, its silent predecessor was shot entirely on location in thirteen weeks in and around New Bedford, Mass., a community saturated with history as an important New England sailing port.

Elmer Clifton, the movie's producer-director and a former assistant-protégé of D. W. Griffith, displays much of that cinemaster's location expertise here, with the result that *Down to the Sea in Ships* displays the physical appearance of a Griffith production. It is quite likely Clifton's best motion picture in a thirty-two year career of directing some eighty-one, mostly undistinguished (and long-forgotten) features.

Clara Bow and James Turfler

Clara Bow and Patrick Hartigan

J. Thornton Baston, William Walcott and Marguerite Courtot.

Down to the Sea in Ships' low budget—financed independently with New England capital—is reflected by the lack of "names" in its cast. Its romantic leads, Marguerite Courtot and Raymond McKee, carried little clout in 1922, and will mean little or nothing to readers of this book. The film's only historically important cast member is Clara Bow, then a seventeen-year-old novice earning $35.00 a week, with only one previous film role to her credit, 1922's *Beyond the Rainbow*. In fact, Bow's amateurish acting in that Billie Dove vehicle had caused her scenes to be removed from the release print. Amusingly, years later, after Bow had become a box-office star, *Beyond the Rainbow* was reissued with Bow's scenes restored.

Set in mid-Nineteenth-Century New England, *Down to the Sea in Ships* centers on a story of thwarted romance and parental manipulation in a Quaker family where the patriarch (William Walcott) sanctions the marriage of his daughter (Marguerite Courtot) to a conniving charlatan (J. Thornton Baston), who has successfully palmed himself off as both a Quaker and a whaling man—two counts of approval not possessed by the girl's true love (Raymond McKee). And although this minor dramatic conflict is pleasingly resolved at the movie's close, it is Bow's exuberant supporting performance as the family mischief-maker (who stows aboard the whaler, disguised as a boy) and the documentary-style whaling sequences that make the picture memorable and worthy of rediscovery. Producer-director Clifton purchased an actual whaling ship for this film, manning it with a real crew of whalers to supplement his cast of professional actors and local extras.

Down to the Sea in Ships previewed in New Bedford in late 1922, but was not generally released until the following year, and was conceded to be among the outstanding pictures of 1923.

DRUMS OF FATE

1923

CREDITS

A Paramount Picture. A Famous Players-Lasky Production. Directed by Charles Maigne. Screenplay by Will M. Ritchey. Based on the novel *Sacrifice* by Stephen French Whitman. Photographed by James (Wong) Howe. Six reels.

CAST

Mary Miles Minter (*Carol Dolliver*); Maurice B. Flynn (*Laurence Teck*); George Fawcett (*Felix Brantome*); Robert Cain (*Cornelius Rysbroek*); Casson Ferguson (*David Verne*); Bertram Grassby (*Hamoud Bin-Said*); Noble Johnson (*Native King*).

In the early Twenties, young Mary Miles Minter was second only to Mary Pickford as America's most popular film actress. From 1912, when (under the name of Juliet Shelby) she made her motion picture debut at ten in *The Nurse*, this vaudeville and Broadway stage veteran proved the power of a determined stage mother by allowing her natural blond beauty and pleasant-but-unskilled talent for acting to be exploited by filmmakers. In a movie career that spanned eleven years, Mary Miles Minter (as she was re-named after *The Nurse*) was featured or starred in some fifty pictures, including the very popular *Anne of Green Gables* (1919), *Judy of Rogue's Harbor* (1920) and *Moonlight and Honeysuckle* (1921). Incredible though it may seem in the permissive Eighties, Minter's career was swiftly brought to an end in 1922 with the murder of William Desmond Taylor, a movie director in his mid-forties who had guided four of her most popular recent films, and with whom she was rumored to have been having a love affair. This "romantic alliance," blown out of all proportion by the "yellow" journalism of 1922, suffered most by following on the heels of the scandal that had ruined comedian Roscoe "Fatty" Arbuckle, and sealed Minter's screen fate. She was allowed to complete her Paramount contract, but following the release of *The Trail of the Lonesome Pine* in the spring of 1923, she quietly retired from the spotlight and lived on wealth gained through real-estate holdings. At her death in August 1984, aged eighty-two, the Taylor murder remained unsolved.

Robert Cain, Casson Ferguson, Mary Miles Minter and George Fawcett

Mary Miles Minter and Robert Cain

Mary Miles Minter and Bertram Grassby

Maurice Flynn, Mary Miles Minter and George Fawcett

Drums of Fate, Minter's next-to-last film, was a story derivative of the overworked Enoch Arden theme of a spouse remarrying when she believes that her mate is dead. In this case, Minter is the young wife of explorer Maurice B. Flynn, who is believed to have died in the African jungle. She then innocently commits bigamy by marrying musician Casson Ferguson, and when her husband number one returns to find his place taken by another, he discreetly decides to return to the jungle. But news of all this bigamous confusion reaches the second husband and, apparently, is sufficient to kill him, leaving our heroine to follow her first husband to Africa, where they're eventually reunited. Confusing?

This sort of plot was not the best showcase for Minter's somewhat limited acting talents, but the movie was not without interest and its star looked particularly lovely as photographed—at her personal request—by James Howe (years before he added the "Wong" as a middle name) on his first solo assignment, following five years of apprenticeship. Charles Maigne, who directed this picture, as well as Minter's swan song, *The Trail of the Lonesome Pine*, appears to have found little rapport with his female star. Contemporary film critics had kinder words for character actors George Fawcett and Robert Cain.

Unfortunately, few of Mary Miles Minter's movies survive for re-evaluation today. But her beauty, her youth and her considerable experience with the industry would seem to have insured a long and increasingly more successful screen career, had not the lurid breath of scandal ruined her at twenty-one.

Mary Miles Minter and Casson Ferguson

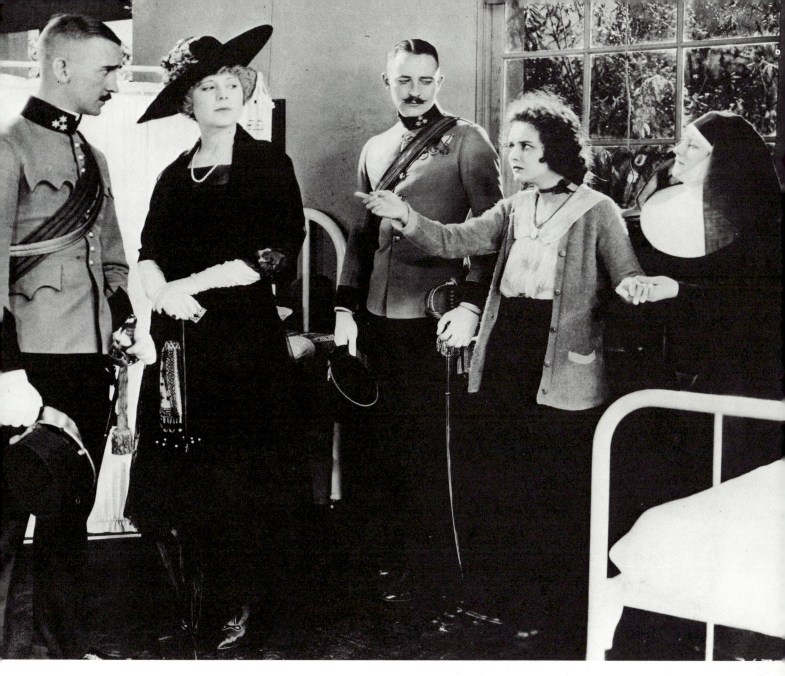

Charles L. King, Dorothy Wallace, Norman Kerry, Mary Philbin and unidentified player

MERRY-GO-ROUND

1923

CREDITS

A Universal Super-Jewel Picture. Presented by Carl Laemmle. Produced by Irving Thalberg. Directed by Rupert Julian and (uncredited) Erich von Stroheim. Screenplay by Finis Fox and (uncredited) Erich von Stroheim, Irving Thalberg and Rupert Julian. Story by Harvey Gates. Titles by Mary O'Hara. Photographed by William Daniels, Ben Reynolds and Charles Kaufman. Edited by Maurice Pivar and James McKay. Art Direction by Richard Day, E. E. Sheeley and Archie Hall. Costumes by Erich von Stroheim and Richard Day. Ten reels.

CAST

Norman Kerry (*Count Franz Maximilian von Hohenegg*); Mary Philbin (*Agnes Urban*); Cesare Gravina (*Sylvester Urban*); Dorothy Wallace (*Countess Gisella von Steinbruck*); Dale Fuller (*Mariana Huber*); George Siegmann (*Schani Huber*); George Hackathorne (*Bartholomew Gruber*); Maude George (*Madame Elvira*); Albert Conti (*Rudi*); Edith Yorke (*Ursula Urban*); Lillian Sylvester (*Aurora Rossreiter*); Al Edmundsen (*Nepomuck Navrital*); Anton Vaverka (*Emperor Franz Josef*); Spottiswoode Aitken (*Minister of War*); Charles L. King (*Nicki*); Jane Sherman (*Maria*); Fenwick Oliver (*Eitel*); Sidney Bracey (*Countess Gisella's Groom*); Helen Broneau (*Jane*).

George Hackathorne and Mary Philbin

George Hackathorne and George Siegmann

Blind Husbands (1919), *The Devil's Passkey* (1920) and *Foolish Wives* (1922) combined to affix Austrian-born writer-director-actor Erich von Stroheim securely on the movieland map, and Universal's chief Carl Laemmle had no reservations about calling the man a "genius" in promoting those films. Russia's great Sergei Eisenstein later hailed Stroheim as "the director of all directors." And yet much of Stroheim's filmmaking career was troubled by his own extravagance, Prussian perfectionism and bullheaded refusal to concede to Hollywood traditions. As a result, his overlong movies were often drastically edited to meet then-standard running-time requirements.

In the case of *Merry-Go-Round*, Stroheim clashed so violently with Universal's production executive Irving Thalberg during the early stages of shooting that he was removed from the film altogether, and replaced by Rupert Julian, one of that studio's "house" directors. Thalberg recast the male lead, which Stroheim was also to have played, with Norman Kerry. In sympathy with Stroheim, actor Wallace Beery then left the chief-villain role, and was, in turn, replaced by George Siegmann. In *Stroheim: A Pictorial Record of His Nine Films* (as a filmmaker), Herman G. Weinberg states that from Stroheim's screenplay, calling for some 1500 scenes, the director had shot 271 (a month's work, at a cost of $220,000) by the time Thalberg halted production in the late summer of 1922. Julian took three additional months to complete the movie, claiming an expenditure of only an additional $170,000. Later, Julian downplayed Stroheim's role in the production of *Merry-Go-Round*, claiming sole credit for the film's direction himself, and belittling his predecessor's contribution to its script and direction. But the Stroheim touch and atmosphere prevail, and certain scenes, experts agree, are definitely the work of Stroheim.

Merry-Go-Round's plot revolves around Count Hohenegg (Norman Kerry), a happy-go-lucky young bachelor attached to the Austrian Emperor's court, and Agnes (Mary Philbin), who works as an organ-grinder in the Prater, Vienna's renowned amusement park. Although engaged to marry Gisella (Dorothy Wallace), the Minister of War's daughter, the Count pretends to be a necktie salesman in order to court Agnes, who, in turn, is secretly loved by Bartholomew (George Hackathorne), a hunchback who also works at the Prater. Because of his feelings for Agnes, the Count makes an unsuccessful effort to break off his engagement to Gisella, whom he is forced to wed. War breaks out, and the Count goes off to fight, encountering Agnes's father, who denounces him before dying among the wounded soldiers. Back in Vienna, Bartholomew wins a lottery and plans to marry Agnes, but before their union can take place, the wounded Count returns. He tells Agnes that his wife has died, thus reuniting the former lovers and leaving Bartholomew to his pet orangutan for consolation. With the coming of spring, the Prater once again comes to life, and the merry-go-round goes on turning.

The critics were impressed with the lavishly produced *Merry-Go-Round*, and praised both its artistry and its cast. *The New York Times* called it "a tense tale of conflicting emotions that will hold any audience," and predicted that it would make a major star of twenty-year-old Mary Philbin, who later re-teamed with Norman Kerry in a pair of 1925 Universal movies, the forgotten melodrama *Fifth Avenue Models* and the Lon Chaney classic *The Phantom of the Opera*.

Wallace MacDonald and Anna Q. Nilsson

THE SPOILERS

1923

CREDITS

A Goldwyn Distributing Corp. Picture. A Jesse D. Hampton Production. Directed by Lambert Hillyer. Screenplay by Fred Kennedy Myton, Elliott Clawson and Hope Loring. Based on the novel by Rex Beach, and the play by Beach and James MacArthur. Photographed by John S. Stumar and Dwight Warren. Eight reels.

CAST

Milton Sills (*Roy Glennister*); Anna Q. Nilsson (*Cherry Malotte*); Barbara Bedford (*Helen Chester*); Robert Edeson (*Joe Dextry*); Ford Sterling (*"Slapjack" Simms*); Wallace MacDonald (*Broncho Kid*); Noah Beery (*Alex McNamara*); Mitchell Lewis (*Marshall Voorhees*); John Elliott (*Bill Wheaton, Attorney*); Robert McKim (*Struve*); Tom McGuire (*Captain Stevens*); Kate Price (*Landlady*); Rockliffe Fellowes (*Matthews*); Gordon Russell (*Burke*); Louise Fazenda (*Tilly Nelson*); Sam De Grasse (*Judge Stillman*); Albert Roscoe (*Mexico Mullins*); Jack Curtis (*Bill Nolan*).

Anna Q. Nilsson and Barbara Bedford

Barbara Bedford and Milton Sills

Over the decades, movie-makers have gained a lot of mileage out of Rex Beach's 1906 novel about Alaska gold-mining, *The Spoilers*. In 1914, the Selig Company first filmed it in a rousingly realistic adaptation featuring William Farnum, Kathlyn Williams and Tom Santschi. Nine years later, Goldwyn released this remake with Milton Sills, Anna Q. Nilsson and Noah Beery.

Producer Jesse D. Hampton's 1923 silent version of *The Spoilers* was directed by Lambert Hillyer, the man behind two of William S. Hart's best 1920 films, *The Toll Gate* and *The Cradle of Courage*, and a top specialist in the area of Hollywood Westerns and action dramas. Basically, this is a faithful adaptation of the Beach novel, tossing all subtlety to the winds, but compensating with good acting, suspense and a wise emphasis on action and the well-observed atmosphere of an ugly, turn-of-the-century Yukon mining town.

The familiar story offers the rugged, popular Milton Sills as Roy Glennister who, with his partner, is victimized by a political deal linked to some Alaskan gold mines. The mine owners, in turn, are being robbed by the corrupt Judge Stillman (Sam De Grasse), in partnership with the town's political boss Alex McNamara (Noah Beery). Along with all this intrigue, there develops a romantic triangle uneasily involving Glennister with Stillman's niece Helen (Barbara Bedford), while dance-hall queen Cherry Malotte (Anna Q. Nilsson) suffers forlornly on the side because of her own unrequited interest in him.

As expected in every adaptation of *The Spoilers*, this one delivers a whopper of a knock-down, drag-out battle royal between Sills and Beery at the story's climax. Despite the renown of 1914's Farnum-Santschi fight sequence, its 1923 equivalent held up very well on its own. In *Variety*, reviewer "Sime." called this one "the corking fight of all time on the screen," and dubbed the picture itself "great work."

Subsequent remakes of the *The Spoilers* have reached the screen, with varying success, in 1930 (Gary Cooper, Betty Compson and William "Stage" Boyd), in 1942 (John Wayne, Marlene Dietrich and Randolph Scott), and—least successful of all—a glossy 1955 Ross Hunter production (Jeff Chandler, Anne Baxter and Rory Calhoun). Perhaps its next incarnation will be as a TV-movie.

Noah Beery, Milton Sills, Anna Q. Nilsson, unidentified player, Ford Sterling, unidentified player, Robert Edeson and Mitchell Lewis.

THE GREEN GODDESS

1923

CREDITS

A Goldwyn-Cosmopolitan Distributing Corp. Picture. A Distinctive Pictures Production. Directed by Sidney Olcott. Screenplay by Forrest Halsey. Based on the play by William Archer. Photographed by Harry Fischbeck. Eight reels.

CAST

George Arliss (*The Rajah of Rukh*); Alice Joyce (*Lucilla Crespin*); Harry T. Morey (*Major Crespin*); David Powell (*Dr. Basil Traherne*); Jetta Goudal (*The Ayah*); Ivan Simpson (*Watkins*); William Worthington (*The High Priest*).

London-born George Arliss was a stage actor of wide experience and distinction by the time he made his first silent motion picture in 1921, at the age of fifty-three. It was an adaptation of *The Devil*, a Molnar play in which he had acted fifteen years earlier, and was followed by other film transcriptions of his stage vehicles, including three which he made twice each, in both silent and sound versions: *Disraeli* (1921 and 1929), *The Man Who Played God* (1922 and 1932) and *The Green Goddess* (1923 and 1930). But of his silent screen career, no film brought Arliss more success than *The Green Goddess*. Critics lavished great praise on his fine performance and Sidney Olcott's meticulous direction. *The New York Times* went so far as to call the movie "a photoplay that shows the dawn of a new era in the motion picture world."

William Archer's 1921 stage melodrama had provided Arliss with an excellent vehicle in both New York and London, as the beturbaned Rajah of Rukh, an Oxford-educated, shrewd but wise-crackingly satirical man of taste and style, even including the affectation of a mono-cle. In cleverness of performance, Arliss's screen competition comes most noticeably from Ivan Simpson, also from the original Broadway cast, in the scene-stealing role of the Rajah's valet. And, to offset the homely and hawkish

Harry T. Morey, David Powell, Alice Joyce, George Arliss and Jetta Goudal

Harry T. Morey, Alice Joyce, George Arliss, Jetta
Goudal and David Powell

George Arliss, Harry T. Morey and Alice Joyce

features of its star, *The Green Goddess* offers beauty in the form of the serenely lovely Alice Joyce and the exotic Jetta Goudal.

Its plot concerns the plight of the British Major Crespin and his wife Lucilla (played by Harry T. Morey and Miss Joyce) who, accompanied by Dr. Traherne (David Powell), the wife's secret lover, have fled a threatening Hindu uprising, only to have their airplane crash into the kingdom of Rukh, where they become the guests of the English-hating Rajah (Arliss). Their quite-civilized host informs the trio that they are also his prisoners, since his three brothers are about to be executed by the British authorities. And he reveals that he intends to kill *them* in retaliation for the imminent death of his siblings. All their efforts to send an appeal for help fail Crespin and Traherne, until the former successfully gets a wireless message through, only to be shot and killed by the Rajah. Ultimately, British fliers arrive to rescue Mrs. Crespin and Traherne.

The Green Goddess was generally considered to be among the ten best films of 1923, but its sound remake failed to get a similar reception in 1930. By then, its melodramatics seemed old-hat, and Arliss's acting more than a little on the hammy side. Thirteen years later, as was their habit, Warner Bros. recycled the old script to bring in a World War II Nazi-Arab conflict, and retitled the story *Adventure in Iraq*, with Paul Cavanagh stepping into the Arliss role and turban. The results were negligible fodder for the supporting-feature market.

TIGER ROSE

1923

CREDITS

A Warner Bros. Picture. Produced by David Belasco. Directed by Sidney Franklin. Screenplay by Edmund Goulding and Millard Webb. Based on the play by Willard Mack. Photographed by Charles Rosher. Eight reels.

CAST

Lenore Ulric (*Rose "Tiger Rose" Bocion*); Forrest Stanley (*Michael Devlin*); Joseph Dowling (*Father Thibault*); Andre de Beranger (*Pierre*); Sam De Grasse (*Dr. Cusick*); Theodore von Eltz (*Bruce Norton*); Claude Gillingwater (*Hector McCollins*).

Lenore Ulric is best remembered today for her lively supporting performance in the Greta Garbo *Camille* of 1937, which marked the forty-four-year-old Ulric's return to the screen, following an eight-year absence. But this darkly exotic, saucer-eyed actress was once an important star of both stage and screen, due largely to the interest taken in her by that legendary showman David Belasco, whom critic Brooks Atkinson once called "the master of mediocrity." Ulric (or "Ulrich," as she originally spelled it) made her film debut in 1911 with the Essanay Company of Chicago, an alliance that continued until she became Belasco's protégée in 1916. Ulric's sultry beauty made her the perfect *femme fatale* in a succession of Belasco stage melodramas with titles like *The Heart of Wetona*, *Kiki* and *Lulu Belle*.

And, although Ulric made few motion pictures during the Twenties, her most notable was *Tiger Rose*, a collaboration between Belasco and Warner Bros. designed to immortalize the actress's 1917 stage characterization. Her mentor had so cunningly tailored that play to her talents that it ran for an amazing 384 performances on Broadway.

As in Willard Mack's stage play, subtitled "a melodrama of the Great Northwest," a Canadian mountie named Michael Devlin (Forrest Stanley) falls in love with wilderness waif Rose Bocion (Ulric) after he's saved her from

Lenore Ulric and Forrest Stanley

Lenore Ulric and Sam De Grasse

Forrest Stanley, Theodore von Eltz, Lenore Ulric and Sam De Grasse

drowning in a rapids. But Rose's heart is with Bruce Norton (Theodore von Eltz), an engineer whom she helps escape imprisonment for killing the man who seduced his sister. Devlin pursues them into the wilderness, but eventually Norton surrenders, serves his sentence and weds Rose.

Sidney Franklin, who had already directed screen versions of such stage hits as *Smilin' Through*, *Dulcy* and *East is West*—and who was known for his taste and style, as well as his success with women stars—made good use of the outdoor locations. And master cameraman Charles Rosher so glorified Ulric with his lighting and close-up artistry that David Belasco sent him a special congrat-

ulatory telegram.

Tiger Rose's success as a silent film moved Warners to remake it with a talking Lupe Velez (and a barking Rin-Tin-Tin) in 1929, the year in which Lenore Ulric herself made a none-too-successful crossover into talkies with a pair of exotic melodramas, *Frozen Justice* and *South Sea Rose*. Belasco's death in 1931 hastened the disintegration of Ulric's career as a star. In the Forties, she found occasional employment as a character actress on both stage and screen. Her last film, in 1947, took Ulric back to the wilderness setting of *Tiger Rose* for the Nelson Eddy-Ilona Massey musical Western, *Northwest Outpost*.

ANNA CHRISTIE

1923

Blanche Sweet

CREDITS

An Associated First National Picture. A Thomas H. Ince Corp. Production. Directed by John Griffith Wray. Screenplay by Bradley King. Based on the stage play by Eugene O'Neill. Photographed by Henry Sharp. Eight reels.

CAST

Blanche Sweet (*Anna Christie*); William Russell (*Matt Burke*); George F. Marion (*Chris Christopherson*); Eugenie Besserer (*Marthy*); Ralph Yearsley (*The Brutal Cousin*); Chester Conklin (*Tommy*); George Siegmann (*Anna's Uncle*); Victor Potel and Fred Kohler (*Bit Players*).

Blanche Sweet and George F. Marion

Between the years 1909 and 1930, Blanche Sweet appeared in at least 122 motion pictures, enjoying popularity as the heroine of a great many early short films of D. W. Griffith, as well as that pioneer director's 1914 four-reel feature *Judith of Bethulia*. Strikingly blond and big-eyed, the actress made some seventy-three movies for the Master before reluctantly leaving Griffith's fold at his recommendation that she accept an offer from producer Jesse Lasky that might broaden her experience—as, indeed, it did. During the Twenties, Sweet proved her versatility in a wide variety of film genres, culminating in what is perhaps her finest dramatic performance, as *Anna Christie*, the past-haunted Swedish-American heroine of Eugene O'Neill's 1921 Pulitzer Prize-winning play. It was brought to the silent screen by Thomas H. Ince, a dynamic producer famed for the high quality of his popular Westerns and melodramas. Years later, Blanche Sweet saluted Ince for his courage in bringing O'Neill's naturalistic work to films: "He pioneered with *Anna*, and I considered it a great honor to pioneer with him."

The action of O'Neill's drama is confined to two settings, a New York waterfront saloon and a section of the coal barge on which the long-separated prostitute Anna and her unsuspecting, seafaring father come to terms with one another. Anna's regeneration eventually appears in the form of a rough-hewn Irish stoker, with whom she falls in love. With George F. Marion repeating his Broadway role as the father, and William Russell as her romantic interest, Blanche Sweet found an unusual congeniality with O'Neill's troubled heroine, inspiring *The New York Times*' anonymous critic to exclaim, "It would be difficult to imagine any actress doing better in this

exacting role." The *Times* also had high praise for the "genius" of actor Marion, as well as director John Griffith Wray's success in handling such a "grim and gripping theme."

Wray also won notice that same year by directing Ince's production of *Human Wreckage*, which tackled the then-daring theme of drug addiction. But he's little remembered today for a directorial career that spanned the Twenties. In 1929, as John Wray, he turned to character acting, in which he continued to his death in 1940, at fifty-two.

In 1930, Greta Garbo made her belated talking-picture debut in a remake of *Anna Christie* that failed to satisfy either Garbo or friends of Eugene O'Neill, who advised him to avoid it. But the playwright did see—and applaud—the silent version, and he made a point to send Blanche Sweet a telegram to express his satisfaction with her fine performance.

Blanche Sweet and Eugenie Besserer.

Irene Rich

LUCRETIA LOMBARD (Flaming Passion)

1923

CREDITS

A Warner Bros. Picture. Produced by Harry Rapf. Directed by Jack Conway. Screenplay by Bertram Milhouser and Sada Cowan. Based on the novel by Kathleen Norris. Seven reels.

CAST

Irene Rich (*Lucretia Morgan*); Monte Blue (*Stephen Winship*); Norma Shearer (*Mimi*); Marc McDermott (*Sir Allen Lombard*); Alec B. Francis (*Judge Winship*); John Roche (*Fred Winship*); Lucy Beaumont (*Mrs. Winship*); Otto Hoffman (*Sandy, Lombard's Servant*).

Incredible romantic complications were often the very essence of Kathleen Norris's best-selling women's fiction, and this adaptation of her novel *Lucretia Lombard* is entirely characteristic. *Variety*'s critic pinned it down appropriately when he assessed the movie "a popular type of picture in which awkward situations are cleared up conveniently by the scenario writer and the director to suit their convenience."

Irene Rich (although she's still known as Lucretia "Morgan" when the story opens) plays the title role of a young woman who, apparently impressed by his title and wealth, weds the much older Sir Allen Lombard (Marc McDermott). Seven years later, Lombard's life of dissipation has left him a drug-ridden wheelchair case, while his young wife loyally attends him and puts up with his abuse. When the old man dies of a drug overdose, accidentally administered by Lucretia, the District Attorney, her neighbor Stephen Winship (Monte Blue), absolves her of blame, and they fall in love. But their happiness is clouded by his father's ward Mimi (Norma Shearer), whom Judge Winship (Alec B. Francis) would have him wed. With his father near death from a shooting accident, Stephen obliges the old man by marrying Mimi, though it's Lucretia whom he still loves. But a dramatic plot twist brings the two women together overnight at a

Norma Shearer and Irene Rich

John Roche, Monte Blue and Norma Shearer

mountain lodge, where a fire breaks out, driving them into the burning forest as Stephen tries to rescue them from an ensuing flood. Finally, Mimi conveniently dies, leaving Stephen free to marry Lucretia.

Rather surprisingly, contemporary critics tended to dismiss *Lucretia Lombard* as cheap, overwrought melodrama (while conceding to the excitement generated by its disaster-climax); and it is true that some of the plotting and Jack Conway's direction strain credibility—especially as regards Mimi's accidental shooting of Judge Winship, whom she (at close range) somehow "mistakes" for a wild animal! But unsubtleties and coincidences abound in a story like this, and *Lucretia Lombard* is best enjoyed for just what it is—a melodramatic love story, well played by the excellent Irene Rich, a most attractive and always believable performer whose warm, ladylike beauty puts one in mind of a brunette Ann Harding. Providing an interesting balance to Rich is the young Norma Shearer, not yet a star but already soundly in possession of that star *quality* that rivets a viewer's attention and makes him remember a performer long after the performance has ended.

In reviewing *Lucretia Lombard*, *Variety* praised Shearer both for her dramatic talents and her looks, and

called her "the find of the cast."

As to the film's other name, Robert E. Sherwood explained it in *Life* magazine: "*Lucretia Lombard*, by the way, has an alternate title, *Flaming Passion*, which is used in those districts where passion is popular."

Norma Shearer and Irene Rich

Glenn Hunter

WEST OF THE WATER TOWER

1923

CREDITS

A Paramount Picture. A Famous Players-Lasky Production. Presented by Adolph Zukor. Directed by Rollin Sturgeon. Screenplay by Doris Schroeder and Lucien Hubbard. Based on the novel by Homer Croy. Photographed by Harry B. Harris. Eight reels.

CAST

Glenn Hunter (*Guy Plummer*); May McAvoy (*Bee Chew*); Ernest Torrence (*The Rev. Adrian Plummer*); George Fawcett (*Charles Chew*); ZaSu Pitts (*Dessie Arnhalt*); Charles Abbe (*R. N. Arnhalt*); Anne Schaefer (*Mrs. Plummer*); Riley Hatch (*Cod Dugan*); Allen Baker (*Ed Hoecker*); Jack Terry (*Harlan Thompson*); Edward Elkas (*Wolfe, the Druggist*); Joseph Burke (*Town Drunk*); Gladys Feldman (*Tootsie*); Alice Mann (*Pal*).

Glenn Hunter and Ernest Torrence

Glenn Hunter was a handsome and popular young stage actor whose biggest success was in *Merton of the Movies*, a Broadway hit of 1922 whose title role he recreated for Hollywood two years later. From 1921 through 1926, Hunter commuted between live theatre and films. But after some sixteen motion pictures—of increasingly diminishing importance—he limited his acting to the stage, where he continued to work sporadically until the end of the Thirties. Upon his death in 1945, at forty-eight, the legend circulated that, having failed to get over a long-ago love affair with actor Alfred Lunt (disrupted by Lynn Fontanne), Hunter had finally died of a broken heart.

In *West of the Water Tower*, the actor co-starred with petite May McAvoy, under the direction of Rollin Sturgeon (*What's Your Daughter Doing?*) in an adaptation of Homer Croy's popular, eyebrow-raising novel, considerably altered to pass the movie censorship standards of 1923, as set down by proprietry czar Will H. Hays.

Its setting is the small Missouri town of Junction City, with its narrow-minded gossips, its unexciting pastimes, its hypocrisy and its adult blandishments to tempt the local young folk. Among those thus influenced are Guy Plummer (played by Hunter), son of the dour-faced Reverend Plummer (Ernest Torrence), a promising youth and Lincoln scholar who listlessly seeks diversion in the town's pool hall and among its looser women. But the girl who finally gets him for a husband—perhaps in defiance of his father—is Bee Chew (McAvoy), daughter of the wealthy agnostic Charles Chew (George Fawcett). Unbelievably, the film's chief dramatic conflict surrounds the arrival of a baby and the inability of Guy and Bee to produce a marriage certificate that would legitimize their offspring. As a result, they face social ostracism and separation, before an eventual happy ending in which the missing document is miraculously produced by the justice of the peace who performed their ceremony.

Sixty-odd years after its release, *West of the Water Tower* is an interesting relic of its era, and with the noteworthy performances of May McAvoy, Ernest Torrence and Glenn Hunter—and its well-observed details of small-town America—it is not undeserving of rediscovery.

Anne Schaefer and Glenn Hunter

Glenn Hunter, May McAvoy and Jack Terry

Charles Abbe, Glenn Hunter,
May McAvoy and unidentified players

Florence Vidor

THE MARRIAGE CIRCLE

1924

CREDITS

A Warner Bros. Picture. Produced and directed by Ernst Lubitsch. Scenario by Paul Bern. Titles by Victor Vance. Based on the play *Nur ein Traum (Only a Dream)* by Lothar Schmidt. Photographed by Charles Van Enger. Art Direction by Lewis Geib and Esdras Hartley. Eight reels.

CAST

Florence Vidor (*Charlotte Braun*); Monte Blue (*Dr. Franz Braun*); Marie Prevost (*Mizzi Stock*); Creighton Hale (*Dr. Gustav Mueller*); Adolphe Menjou (*Prof. Josef Stock*); Harry Myers (*The Detective*); Esther Ralston (*Pauline Hofer*); Dale Fuller (*A Nervous Woman*).

The Marriage Circle, the great German director Ernst Lubitsch's follow-up film to his critically acclaimed American debut with Mary Pickford's *Rosita*, presents (over sixty years after its first screening) a wealth of that subtle wit and adult theatrical invention that have made "the Lubitsch touch" legendary.

In its day, *The Marriage Circle* was a landmark in American motion-picture comedy and a welcome departure from the broad slapstick farces of the early Twenties. Here, through clever scripting and a brilliant combination of acting and direction, the comedy-of-manners reached its apex on the silent screen. *The Marriage Circle* offers bedroom farce portrayed without resorting to overemphasis or overstepping the bounds of good taste. There is nothing here to offend the unwary, but neither does it underestimate or insult the intelligence of an adult audience. And its plot developments are enacted with such knowing clarity by a small but eloquent cast that the movie's paucity of intertitles is barely noticeable.

Misunderstandings, confusions of identity and imagined marital transgressions spin the somewhat involved plotline of this adaptation by Paul Bern of a German stage play by Lothar Schmidt. But keen portrayals of character

Adolphe Menjou and Marie Prevost

Marie Prevost and Monte Blue

Monte Blue and Florence Vidor

Monte Blue and Marie Prevost

always keep the film's audience clear as to who's doing what to whom: Marie Prevost's ever-scheming minx of a faithless wife; Adolphe Menjou, her suave, grounds-seeking ex-husband-to-be; Monte Blue, the confused but loving husband momentarily sidetracked by Prevost; Florence Vidor, the devoted, trusting wife who's devastated to find that her husband (Blue) and best woman-friend (Prevost) have been trysting behind her back; and Creighton Hale, the bachelor-friend out to snare a wife—*anyone's* wife!

Lubitsch's distinctive imprint on *The Marriage Circle* is woven throughout this marvelous comedy as occasional close-ups underscore such telling observations of character as a hand striking the keys of a piano in expression of surprise, or a skillful intercutting of facial reactions to a plot-turn not fully understood by all of a scene's characters. Fortunately, all of Lubitsch's hand-picked cast well knew what they were about, and the resultant movie classic set a precedent for all subsequent attempts at sophisticated comedy on the American screen.

THE THIEF OF BAGDAD

1924

Snitz Edwards and Douglas Fairbanks

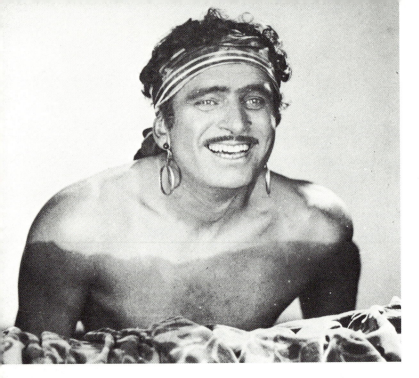

Douglas Fairbanks.

CREDITS

A United Artists Picture. A Douglas Fairbanks Pictures Corp. Production. Directed by Raoul Walsh. Assistant Director: James T. O'Donohoe. Screenplay by Elton Thomas (Douglas Fairbanks). Scenario Editor: Lotta Woods. Photographed by Arthur Edeson. Edited by William Nolan. Art Direction by William Cameron Menzies, assisted by Irvin J. Martin, Anton Grot, Paul Youngblood, H. R. Hopps, Harold W. Grieve, Park French, William Utwich and Edward Langley. Costumes by Mitchell Leisen. Special Effects by Hampton Del Ruth. Technical Director: Robert Fairbanks. Twelve reels.

CAST

Douglas Fairbanks (*The Thief of Bagdad*); Snitz Edwards (*His Evil Associate*); Charles Belcher (*The Holy Man*); Julanne Johnston (*The Princess*); Anna May Wong (*The Mongol Slave*); Winter-Blossom (*The Slave of the Lute*); Etta Lee (*The Slave of the Sand Board*); Brandon Hurst (*The Caliph*); Tote Du Crow (*His Soothsayer*); Sojin (*The Mongol Prince*); K. Nambu (*His Counselor*); Sadakichi Hartmann (*His Court Magician*); Noble Johnson (*The Indian Prince*); M. Comont (*The Persian Prince*); Charles Stevens (*His Awaker*); Sam Baker (*The Sworder*); Jess Weldon, Scott Mattraw and Charles Sylvester (*The Eunuchs*).

The Thief of Bagdad was Douglas Fairbanks' most ambitious production and, filmed at a cost of nearly $2,000,000, his most expensive as well. His 1922 *Robin Hood* had cost $700,000 to make, and had brought in more than $3,000,000 at the box-office. But *The Thief of Bagdad* was not so successful with the Fairbanks public. Perhaps it was too ambitious in concept, with its star a bit dwarfed by all of the spectacular Art Nouveau sets and special effects. And probably the movie's canvas was too large and sprawling to captivate its audience. Running in excess of two and a half hours, this (for its era) ultimate Arabian Nights adventure-fantasy tried to cram in too much and, in so doing, tired its spectators. There are just too many grandiose settings designed by the talented William Cameron Menzies, and there are too many episodes to flesh out the convoluted and very episodic plot. One loses track of where one is in the story, and just when it all seems about to resolve itself, away the story travels in another direction.

Douglas Fairbanks and Julanne Johnston

Tote Du Crow, Sojin and Julanne Johnston

But with all its excesses, *The Thief of Bagdad* is a beautiful film and one worthy of respect. For Doug's fans, it must have been something of a letdown in 1924 to witness their favorite's athletic cavortings of a type more balletic than gymnastic (as in his previous efforts), as though he had been studying Nijinsky's performance in *The Spectre of the Rose*. The first third of the movie offers Fairbanks clad in harem pajamas with his tightly-muscled, tanned upper torso bare. Here he's constantly in motion, performing superhuman, magical leaps and bounds— sometimes with the aid of unseen trampolines or suspended piano wire. Later, disguised as a prince, he's clad from head to toe in satins, earrings and pearl necklaces— hardly the Doug Fairbanks image to which his adulators were accustomed.

When *The Thief* was in production, Fairbanks was tremendously influenced by the epic pictures emanating from the studios of Germany, such as Fritz Lang's *Der Müde Tode* (1921). In fact, the actor purchased U.S. rights to that fantasy film, and held up its Stateside release while instructing his artisans to duplicate some of its magical touches in his own current motion picture. Consequently, it features winged horses, flying carpets and armies which wondrously increase a hundredfold within the space of a few minutes. No cost was spared to create each and every new illusion that crossed the Fairbanks mind, with the result that Doug-the-performer was often quite swamped by Doug-the-producer. There was the beautiful, veiled princess (Julanne Johnston, who was little more than a luscious Maxfield Parrish painting come to passive life), the sinister-looking Mongol prince (the always-villainous Oriental actor Sojin), the Thief's lively sidekick (Snitz Edwards) and the villain's lovely slave-girl pawn (sixteen-year-old Anna May Wong in a role that attracted considerable attention at the time). And even today, after the scores of Arabian Nights adventure films that have emerged from the studios of Hollywood in the course of sixty intervening years, much of the cinematic magic in the 1924 *Thief* still causes one to marvel at the facility with which it is all deployed.

The Thief of Bagdad did meet with commercial success, though nowhere the equal of previous Fairbanks vehicles, and never again did the actor attempt to provide himself with so elaborate a showcase. Instead, he next played it safe with a sequel (*Don Q, Son of Zorro*), followed by a swashbuckler (*The Black Pirate*).

UNGUARDED WOMEN

1924

CREDITS

A Paramount Picture. A Famous Players-Lasky Production. Presented by Adolph Zukor and Jesse L. Lasky. Directed by Alan Crosland. Scenario by James Ashmore Creelman. Based on Lucy Stone Terrill's story *Face*, as published in *The Saturday Evening Post*. Photographed by Henry Cronjager. Six reels.

CAST

Bebe Daniels (*Breta Banning*); Richard Dix (*Douglas Albright*); Mary Astor (*Helen Castle*); Walter McGrail (*Larry Trent*); Frank Losee (*George Castle*); Helen Lindroth (*Aunt Louise*); Harry Mestayer (*Sing Woo*); Donald Hall (*James Craig*); Joe King (*Capt. Robert Banning*).

In light of current filmmaking trends, it's a rare year that offers one of our current crop of stars in more than one or perhaps two movies. But in the mid-Twenties, it was commonplace to find popular players like Bebe Daniels, Richard Dix and Mary Astor working in an average of six or seven motion pictures in any twelve-month period. At Paramount, where the annual volume of films was considerable throughout the decade, the average product was produced, photographed and packaged with a high degree of professionalism, with dramas and comedies of the standard "program" variety outdistancing the occasional super-productions like *The Ten Commandments*, *Monsieur Beaucaire* and *Peter Pan*.

Unguarded Women was just one of fifty-six movies that Paramount released in 1924, with established favorites Daniels and Dix in an Oriental-set romantic drama of star-crossed relationships, with beautiful, eighteen-year-old Mary Astor as the quiet, sideline-fiancée whose patience rewards her with hero Dix at the film's close.

Guilt and obligation motivate the character portrayed here by Dix. A World War I veteran, he's conscience-stricken by the fact that he feels responsible for his

Bebe Daniels

Mary Astor and Richard Dix

buddy's battleground death, the result of disorientation under fire. Being honored at an Armistice Day anniversary gathering drives Dix to China in search of his late friend's widow (Daniels), who's now leading so fast and undisciplined a life that she's lost "face" among the other members of the foreign colony. Especially controversial is her relationship with the dissolute Walter McGrail, and Dix determines he owes it to the woman and her husband's memory to redeem her. As a result, he's bent on *marrying* Daniels, even though it means forsaking his own gorgeous fiancée (Astor), a rather drastic step that might seem difficult for an audience to accept were the role acted by less persuasive an actor than Richard Dix.

The story's denouement witnesses a regeneration in the Daniels character when she discovers that Dix is acting purely out of a sense of duty, and sacrificing his love for Astor to wed her. To prevent further unhappiness for those in her orbit, Daniels commits suicide.

With the seasoned skill of Bebe Daniels and the poised sincerity of young Mary Astor to lend conviction to this unlikely melodrama, director Alan Crosland managed to make this a film of strength and substance. For posterity, however, his name will be better recognized for Barrymore's *Don Juan* (1926) and Jolson's *The Jazz Singer* (1927).

Mary Astor, Harry Mestayer, Bebe Daniels and Richard Dix

THE NAVIGATOR

1924

Buster Keaton

CREDITS

A Metro-Goldwyn-Mayer Picture. Presented by Joseph M. Schenck. Directed by Donald Crisp and Buster Keaton. Story and titles by Jean Havez, Clyde Bruckman and Joseph Mitchell. Photographed by Elgin Lessley and Byron Houck. Technical direction by Fred Gabourie. Six reels.

CAST

Buster Keaton (*Rollo Treadway*); Kathryn McGuire (*Betsy O'Brien*); Frederick Vroom (*"Cappy" John O'Brien, Her Father*). With Noble Johnson, Clarence Burton, H. M. Clugston, and the liner S.S. *Buford*.

Buster Keaton and Kathryn McGuire

Dour, stone-faced Buster Keaton enjoys a well-deserved position high among the screen's all-time comic geniuses, especially for his work in that soundless golden era of pantomimic farce.

Like most of his colleagues, Buster began in short comedies produced in the prolific Teens, moving on to achieve his greatest fame in the silent features in which he starred during the Twenties, including *The Three Ages* (1923), *Sherlock, Jr.* (1924), *Seven Chances* (1925) and—the one for which he's best remembered—that classic Civil War comedy, *The General* (1927).

Among the comedian's unique characteristics was a brilliant talent for comic invention of the most physical sort, without recourse to the sentimental ploys which flawed some of the work of his rival contemporaries. Buster later expressed impatience with those who would explain or analyze the Keaton style, commenting: "What you have to do is create a character. Then the character just does his best, and there's your comedy. No begging."

In his well-received 1979 biography *Keaton*, Tom Dardis claims that *The Navigator* was the comedian's personal *second* favorite of all his films (next to *The General*), as well as the first Keaton feature to achieve wide popularity. Sixty years later, it still generates hearty laughter for its sustained and timeless visual humor.

The Navigator's genesis lay in Keaton's decision to buy, for $25,000, the S.S. *Buford*, a has-been passenger ship destined for the wreckers. Having purchased the boat, he then gathered his creative associates together and put them to the question, "What could we do with an ocean liner?" The answer they contrived to work from: the *Buford* would be a "dead" ship, without lights or running

water, and Keaton would be stranded on it with the girl he is determined (against her will) to marry.

Aside from Keaton and leading lady Kathryn McGuire, *The Navigator* has few other characters of importance—except, of course, the *Buford*. And most of the film's action takes place on shipboard, where wealthy, doltish Rollo Treadway and pretty but ineffectual Betsy O'Brien spend a lot of hilarious footage just missing one another, via split-second comic timing, as they simultaneously explore the deserted vessel. Subsequent humor derives from such gag routines as Buster's efforts to make them breakfast (using salt water for the coffee), a bout with a folding chair that defies being sat on, and a climax involving Rollo and Betsy with cannibals on an island. Making this film evidently provided a rugged physical workout for Keaton, including much dunking in the water and an undersea sequence in which he's in a diving suit, engaged in a wild swordfish fuel, with *him* brandishing one of the two *fish*!

Keaton collaborated on the movie's direction with veteran actor Donald Crisp, and its huge success won him a lucrative new contract with Metro-Goldwyn-Mayer, calling for him to produce and star in two films a year at $27,000 per finished product.

But with the coming of talkies, Buster's star waned; he was never as eloquent with dialogue as with pantomime, and eventually he sank to comic supporting roles that capitalized on his frozen-faced humor and established name.

FORBIDDEN PARADISE

1924

CREDITS

A Paramount Picture. A Famous Players-Lasky Production. Presented by Jesse L. Lasky and Adolph Zukor. Directed by Ernst Lubitsch. Screenplay by Hans Kraly and Agnes Christine Johnson. Based on the play *The Czarina* by Lajos Biro and Melchior Lengyel. Photographed by Charles Van Enger. Sets by Hans Dreier. Eight reels.

CAST

Pola Negri (*Catherine, the Czarina*); Rod La Rocque (*Capt. Alexei Czerny*); Adolphe Menjou (*Chancellor*); Pauline Starke (*Anna*); Fred Malatesta (*French Ambassador*); Nick de Ruiz (*The General*); Carrie D'Aumery (*Lady-in-Waiting*); Clark Gable (*Extra*).

Rod La Rocque and Pola Negri

Ernst Lubitsch had already directed Pola Negri in six of her early German films, including *Carmen* (1918) and *Madame Dubarry* (1919), when he was assigned to her seventh American vehicle, *Forbidden Paradise*. It's still among the actress's best movies, underscoring the reasons for Lubitsch's being her favorite director. An adaptation of the Lajos Biro-Melchior Lengyel stage play *The Czarina* (later to provide the basis also for 1945's *A Royal Scandal*, with Tallulah Bankhead), *Forbidden Paradise* updates the original work to eliminate all references to its central figure's actually being Russia's Catherine the Great. In the movie, the period is contemporary Twenties and the locale an unspecified European kingdom. Lacking any reference to "Mother Russia" and the like, the screenplay nevertheless depicts a Queen Catherine (portrayed by Negri) who harbors a healthy interest in men, especially those who are new to her circle. And, in this film, her interest is mainly directed toward a young army officer named Alexei (Rod La Rocque) who arrives one day to warn of revolutionary conspirators threatening the future of her small kingdom. Ignoring the advances of the visiting French Ambassador, Catherine determines to

Pauline Starke and Pola Negri

Adolphe Menjou and Pola Negri

seduce the officer. But the situation is immediately complicated by the fact that his sweetheart is Catherine's lady-in-waiting Anna (Pauline Starke). But Alexei is flattered by the Czarina's attentions, and deserts Anna for Catherine's boudoir, only to discover that he's not the only man in her affections. In retaliation, he joins the revolutionists plotting her overthrow. But the Chancellor quells the revolution, and the Czarina has Alexei arrested. Later, she relents and releases him from prison, allowing him to reconcile with Anna. As the movie closes, Catherine has entered into a new affair—with the French Ambassador.

There were probably few directors capable of bringing off such potentially racy material with the sly deftness of a Lubitsch, who had already demonstrated his skill with sex farce in *The Marriage Circle*. But he manages the textual winks and innuendoes so smoothly that adult members of his audience cannot fail to get the point, while those of younger or less sophisticated mentality might miss these naughty subtleties altogether. In short, the perfect example of how a clever Hollywood director could mollify the censorship demands of the Will Hays Office without completely compromising his motion picture. Lubitsch went on to please critics and audiences alike for the remainder of the decade with such popular films as *Lady Windermere's Fan* (1925), *The Student Prince* (1927) and *The Love Parade* (1929).

Pola Negri, on the other hand, never quite managed to become the popular American luminary she had once been in Germany. Perhaps her European exoticism was too heavy for Anglo-Saxon audiences. In a way, Negri had stepped into the vamping man-killer roles played earlier by Theda Bara. Pola's colorfully vital acting later moved film historian Lotte Eisner to call her "The Magnani of the Silent Screen." *Forbidden Paradise* is reputed to have been Negri's favorite among all of her films.

ISN'T LIFE
WONDERFUL

1924

Neil Hamilton

D.W. Griffith

CREDITS

A United Artists Picture. A D. W. Griffith Production. Produced, directed and written for the screen by D. W. Griffith. Based on the short story by Maj. Geoffrey Moss in his book *Defeat*. Photographed by Hendrick Sartov and Hal Sintzenich. Nine reels.

CAST

Carol Dempster (*Inga*); Neil Hamilton (*Paul*); Helen Lowell (*The Grandmother*); Erville Alderson (*The Professor*); Frank Puglia (*Theodor*); Lupino Lane (*Rudolph*); Marcia Harris (*The Aunt*); Hans von Schlettow (*Leader of the Hungry Laborers*); Paul Rehkopf and Robert Scholz (*Hungry Laborers*); Walter Plimmer, Jr. (*The American*).

In 1924, D. W. Griffith, choosing art over commercialism, defied any facile bid for box-office popularity by taking a small cast and crew to Germany, where he shot the many atmospheric exterior scenes for a documentary-style drama called *Isn't Life Wonderful*. Social realism wasn't usually Griffith's forte, but this stark, if eternally optimistic, story of a Polish family struggling to survive amid the desperate poverty and inflation of post-World War I Germany certainly bears the ring of truth. And lest one surmise that the film's title is an ironic one, it echoes the Pollyanna-like sentiments of the heroine as she continually surmounts adversity to count her blessings. The movie wouldn't bear the Griffith trademark if it didn't have some sentiment. However, *extreme* sentimentality is mercifully absent.

Isn't Life Wonderful was the director's last picture as an independent filmmaker before folding his studios in Mamaroneck, New York, and going to work for Paramount Pictures. In her memoir, *The Movies, Mr. Griffith and Me*, Lillian Gish reflected upon this movie's failure in America, while praising its artistry. "It was the only picture he made after I left him," she wrote, "that I thought worthy of him."

Based on a short story by the British Maj. Geoffrey Moss, the film tells of a Polish refugee family living in a cramped apartment in a Berlin suburb circa 1918–23. They are a grandmother (Helen Lowell) confined to her wheelchair; the elderly professor (Erville Alderson), who corrects exam papers; his older son Paul (Neil Hamilton), who returns home from the war weakened from the effects of poison gas; the young son Theodor (Frank

Carol Dempster and Neil Hamilton

Puglia), who waits on tables in a nightclub; an aunt (Marcia Harris); Inga (Carol Dempster), an adopted daughter who works in a shop and is in love with Paul; and an out-of-work entertainer named Rudolph (Lupino Lane) whom they've taken in. Their impoverished household customarily gathers at an evening meal of steamed turnips and nothing else. Which results in the movie's most heartwarming scene, when unexpected good fortune makes it possible for the family's younger members to surprise their elders with potatoes, a freshly laid egg— and a coveted liverwurst!

Paul and Inga want to get married, but the reality of their poverty prevents the immediate realization of that dream. Obtaining a small tract of land, he plants potatoes and sets about secretly building them a little house. But their path to this goal isn't smooth. The community is close to starvation, and a group of unemployed laborers show their resentment of those who "have" by going after whomever they think is profiteering in food. As a result, our hero and heroine, having exhausted themselves harvesting a large potato crop, are set upon by this starving band, attacked and robbed of all their potatoes— but celebrate their joy in still having one another. The movie ends on an upbeat note when, after the passage of a year (and an apparent upswing in the German economy), the newlyweds are showing their new home to the joyous family.

Griffith shot *Isn't Life Wonderful*'s interior scenes back home in Mamaroneck. But much of the story takes place outdoors, and the authentic look of all those locations fully makes up for the difficulties he must have encountered in July and August of 1924, when he filmed in the streets of Old Berlin, the shipyard at Kopenick, the forests of Sacrow and Crampnitz and the potato gardens at Grunau.

All of the movie's cast does fine work, but especially memorable are Carol Dempster and Neil Hamilton—she with her thin, wanly attractive plainness, and he strained with the agonized memories of war coupled with the survival problems of a ravaged and depressed economy. Faced with the bleakest of futures, neither will accept defeat. They are survivors.

Dempster, in her brief career as a movie star, worked almost exclusively with Griffith, who was apparently very much taken with her. *Isn't Life Wonderful* presents this usually vivacious, pretty actress in shabby clothing, a severe hair style and the plainest of make-ups, and the

Neil Hamilton, Erville Alderson, Helen Lowell, Marcia Harris and Carol Dempster.

result is a haunting performance which Dempster never surpassed. Neil Hamilton's quiet steadfastness and solid masculinity never obtrude, which perhaps helps to explain why this handsome and sensitive actor, who enjoyed a lengthy career, never quite became the important leading man a bit more charisma would have insured. Very much the sum total of its parts, *Isn't Life Wonderful* remains an unforgettable cinema landmark of the Twenties.

Hans von Schlettow, Paul Rehkopf, Robert Scholz, Neil Hamilton and Carol Dempster.

Ronald Colman and Constance Talmadge

HER SISTER FROM PARIS

1925

CREDITS

A First National Picture. Produced by Joseph M. Schenck. Directed by Sidney Franklin. Assistant Director: Scot R. Beal. Screenplay by Hans Kraly. Photographed by Arthur Edeson. Art Direction by William Cameron Menzies. Costumes by Adrian. Seven reels.

CAST

Constance Talmadge (*Helen Weyringer/Lola, known as "La Perry"*); Ronald Colman (*Joseph Weyringer*); George K. Arthur (*Robert Well*); Margaret Mann (*Bertha*); Gertrude Claire.

Ronald Colman, Constance Talmadge and George K. Arthur

Of the three Brooklyn-born Talmadge sisters, Norma, the eldest, was best at heart-tugging melodrama; Natalie was a minor-league silent-comedy actress, best known as the wife of Buster Keaton; and Constance, the youngest, was almost unrivaled in the field of sophisticated film comedy.

Constance Talmadge got started in motion pictures in 1914 in her early teens, playing in many of the shorts of debonair comedian Billy Quirk, before breaking into the big time as the lively Mountain Girl of Griffith's epic *Intolerance* (1916). Nowhere near as prolific as many of her contemporaries, Constance apparently was too busy enjoying a hectic social life to make more than two or three films a year during the Twenties. Four times wed, Constance was seldom idle during the in-between gaps; according to her friend Dorothy Gish, "Constance was always getting engaged—but never to less than two men at the same time."

During 1925, Constance Talmadge found the time to make a pair of movie comedies, *Learning to Love* and *Her Sister From Paris*, the latter reteaming her with Ronald Colman, the actress's leading man from the previous year's amusing *Her Night of Romance*. In their 1925 showcase, a rather risqué sex farce, they portray Helen and Joseph Weyringer, a Viennese couple whose marriage has grown stale. The husband, a well-known author, has become bored, and his attitude drives her from him. But a meeting with her twin sister, the famed dancer Lola, changes things when she helps Helen make herself over in an effort to regain Joseph's interest. Helen returns home posing as "Lola," and immediately gains the attention of both Joseph and his best friend, Robert (George K. Arthur). The situation waxes complicated as Helen/Lola "seduces" her own husband, eventually letting him in on the truth, introducing him to her *real* Parisian sister, and reawakening her husband's love for herself.

This "naughty" situation reportedly upset certain state censorship boards, prompting First National to do a bit of re-editing prior to general release of the movie. But the situation remained titillating, nevertheless, and audiences were properly amused, especially with the opportunity of seeing *two* Constance Talmadges, literally performing beside themselves, courtesy of some clever trick photography. Sidney Franklin, who had guided Talmadge and Colman through *Her Night of Romance*, again directed them here and, although lacking the sly approach of a Lubitsch, managed this comedy with success. His female star later credited Colman's presence with inspiring her to try a little harder to give of her best.

Her Sister from Paris's plot will sound familiar to movie buffs; its basic premise was later used for *Moulin Rouge* (1934) and Garbo's unfortunate swan song *Two-Faced Woman* (1941).

THE GOLD RUSH

1925

Charlie Chaplin

Georgia Hale and Charlie Chaplin

CREDITS

A United Artists Picture. A Charlie Chaplin Production. Produced, directed and written by Charlie Chaplin. Associate Director: Charles "Chuck" F. Reisner. Assistant Directors: Harry D'Abbadie D'Arrast and (uncredited) Edward Sutherland. Photographed by Roland H. Totheroh. Camera Assistant: Jack Wilson. Production Manager: Alfred Reeves. Nine reels (copyrighted at ten reels).

CAST

Charlie Chaplin (*The Lone Prospector*); Mack Swain (*Big Jim McKay*); Tom Murray (*Black Larson*); Georgia Hale (*The Girl*); Malcolm Waite (*Jack Cameron*); Betty Morrisey (*The Girl's Friend*); Henry Bergman (*Hank Curtis*).

The Gold Rush is widely hailed in many quarters as the greatest masterpiece of that genius of motion picture comedy, Charlie Chaplin. It's also the film for which, he once said, he'd like to be remembered. And so he will, for *The Gold Rush* cunningly blends hilarious comic slapstick with melodramatic thrills, and not a little bit of pathos. It

was Charlie's longest movie to that date, as well as his most painstaking effort, reproducing Alaska's Chilkoot Pass in Nevada's Rocky Mountains, at an approximate production cost of $600,000.

Chaplin's scenario is said to have been inspired by the terrible ordeal of the 1840's Donner Party, pioneers stranded in the wintry mountains and moved to acts of cannibalism for survival. But, of course, *Charlie's* references to snowbound hunger and desperation were all aimed at *humor*. The closest *The Gold Rush* ever approaches anything as desperate as cannibalism is the scene in which a starving Mack Swain twice hallucinates that his cabin-mate, Chaplin, is a giant chicken—with Swain's appropriate lick-smacking in anticipation of a tasty meal. Otherwise, the movie mines more positive comic elements in the "gold fever" that drove men to battle the Alaskan climate for the dim possibility of wealth.

Charlie's "Lone Prospector" (the character has no name) is little more than his world-famous "Little Tramp" character, transplanted to Alaska, with only a pair of worn gloves and a lightweight shawl as unlikely protection against the cold. But there's still the trademark mustache, baggy pants, bowler hat and bamboo cane to help ward

Tom Murray and Charlie Chaplin

Charlie Chaplin, Tom Murray and Mack Swain

off any tendency audiences might have to take *The Gold Rush* seriously.

The film is quite nearly plotless. The Prospector befriends a burly fellow-prospector Big Jim McKay (Mack Swain), who has already struck it rich, thus becoming the target of desperado Black Larson (Tom Murray). The latter is eventually dispatched via an avalanche. Our hero also falls in love with a dance-hall girl (Georgia Hale), who appears only to toy with his emotions, but whom he eventually wins, after he and his pal McKay have become millionaires.

The Gold Rush has its slow moments, but its memorable comic "set-pieces" more than compensate: the "gourmet" cooked-boot dinner, shared by Chaplin and Swain; the imaginary New Year's Eve dinner party at which the Prospector entertains his girlfriend with a pair of dancing rolls; and the nail-biting climax wherein Mack and Charlie awaken to find their storm-blown little cabin teetering on the edge of a precipice.

Eddie Sutherland, who apprenticed under Chaplin on both *A Woman of Paris* and *The Gold Rush* before becoming a director in his own right, has recalled, "It took us weeks to cook up the routine when Chaplin eats his boots. The shoelaces were made of licorice; so were the shoes. The nails were some kind of candy. We had something like twenty pairs of boots made by a confectioner, and we shot and shot that scene, too. Charlie ate it as if it were the most sumptuous meal served at the Astor. He knew that an audience liked a character to play against himself; if the character was shabby, he should act in a very genteel manner."

Sutherland claims he left *The Gold Rush*, still in production, after some eighteen months, at which time he recalled perfectionist Chaplin as being only about two-thirds of the way toward completion. "But of course he didn't shoot all the time," explained the former assistant-director. "We'd shoot for three or four days, then lay off for a couple of weeks and rethink, rehearse, and rarefy the scene." Such perfectionism as this kept Charlie Chaplin's feature-film output down to only one other Twenties release, 1928's *The Circus* (the Thirties witnessed only *two* new Chaplin films, *City Lights* and *Modern Times*).

The Gold Rush was an immediate box-office hit when it opened in the late summer of 1925, more than compensating Chaplin for all the time and money expended on his efforts. Charlie always retained control of his feature films, and in 1942 he re-edited and reissued *The Gold Rush* in a "tightened" form, for which he composed a musical score and spoke the narration. Again, this silent movie was a hit, confirming its status as a Chaplin classic.

*Mack Swain and
Charlie Chaplin*

*Charlie Chaplin,
Georgia Hale
and Malcolm
Waite.*

GR-58

THE MERRY WIDOW

1925

CREDITS

A Metro-Goldwyn-Mayer release of an Erich von Stroheim Production. Directed by Erich von Stroheim. Assistant Directors: Edward Sowders and Louis Germonprez. Adaptation and scenario by Erich von Stroheim and Benjamin Glazer. Based on the operetta *Die Lustige Witwe*, libretto by Leo Stein and Victor Leon. Titles by Marian Ainslee. Photographed by Oliver Marsh, William Daniels and Ben Reynolds. Technicolor sequence photographed by Ray Rennahan. Edited by Frank Hull and (uncredited) Irving Thalberg. Art Direction by Cedric Gibbons and Richard Day. Costume supervision by Erich von Stroheim and Richard Day. Original score by David Mendoza and William Axt, after the music of Franz Lehar. Ten reels.

CAST

Mae Murray (*Sally O'Hara*); John Gilbert (*Prince Danilo*); Roy D'Arcy (*Crown Prince Mirko*); Tully Marshall (*Baron Sadoja*); Josephine Crowell (*Queen Milena*); George Fawcett (*King Nikita*); Albert Conti (*Danilo's Adjutant*); Wilhelm von Brincken (*Danilo's Aide-de-Camp*); Sidney Bracey (*Danilo's Footman*); Don Ryan (*Mirko's Adjutant*); Hughie Mack (*Innkeeper*); Ida Moore (*Innkeeper's Wife*); Lucille van Lent (*Innkeeper's Daughter*); Charles Margelis (*Flo Epstein*); Harvey Karels (*Jimmy Watson*); Edna Tichenor (*Dopey Marie*); Gertrude Bennett (*Hard-Boiled Virginia*); Zalla Zarana (*Frenchie Christine*); Jacqueline Gadsdon (*Madonna*); Estelle Clark (*French Barber*); D'Arcy Corrigan (*Horatio*); Clara Wallucks and Frances Primm (*Hansen Sisters*); Zack Williams (*George Washington White*); Eugene Pouget (*François*); Edward Connelly (*Ambassador*); Meriwyn Thayer (*Ambassador's Wife*); George Nichols (*Doortender at François'*); Dale Fuller (*Sally's Maid*); Lon Poff (*Sadoja's Lackey*); Anielka Elter (*Blindfolded Musician*); Carolynne Snowden (*Black Dancer*); Louise Hughes, Anna Maynard, Helen Howard Beaumont and Beatrice O'Brien (*Chorus Girls*).

John Gilbert and Mae Murray

Blond Mae Murray, whose film career spanned the years 1917 to 1931, was famed for her "bee-stung" lips, coy mannerisms and penchant for dance numbers in her screen vehicles—even when they seemed scarcely appropriate to the dramatic content of the picture. A former Ziegfeld girl, she was frequently the star of movies directed by her husband Robert Z. Leonard for Tiffany, their own production company, which, in the early Twenties, released through Metro Pictures. In 1924, when the latter merged into Metro-Goldwyn-Mayer, the new corporation was only too happy to acquire a top box-office attraction like Murray and star her in producer-director Erich von Stroheim's adaptation (with co-author Benjamin Glazer) of Franz Lehar's 1906 operetta *The Merry Widow*. But since this film was, of course, silent, there was little to attract operetta buffs (although the David Mendoza-William Axt score did offer cinema pianists accompanying this film the opportunity to touch upon such Lehar melodies as "The Merry Widow Waltz"). And von Stroheim's screenplay veered far from the original Leo Stein-Victor Leon libretto, changing the show's title-character from the wealthy Marsovian widow Sonia to a touring American showgirl named Sally O'Hara (Mae Murray), who marries a wealthy, old nobleman, the degenerate Baron Sadoja (Tully Marshall), after being jilted by Danilo (John Gilbert), a handsome young officer. Since Danilo is actually a prince, and second in line to the throne of Monteblanco, a marriage between them is strictly forbidden. But the baron dies of locomotor ataxia on his wedding night, thus leaving Sally not only widowed, but both rich and merry. In Paris, she becomes the envied object of general desire, not least among them both Danilo and his lecherous older brother, the Crown Prince Mirko (smirking Roy D'Arcy), who duel over Sally. Danilo is wounded, drawing Sally's sympathy; the elderly King (George Fawcett), dies, and the unpopular Mirko is assassinated at his father's state funeral. All of which finally leaves Danilo and Sally to wed and become King and Queen of Monteblanco, as the movie switches from monochrome to full 1925 Technicolor for their coronation procession.

Lavishly produced and artfully photographed by William Daniels, Ben Reynolds and Mae Murray's favorite cameraman Oliver Marsh (whose clever lighting made the thirty-five-year-old actress's face look more youthful), *The Merry Widow* won high critical praise and became one of 1925's most popular motion pictures. The finished product bore no scars of the bitter von Stroheim-Murray feud which had constantly plagued the movie's lengthy, fourteen-week shooting schedule. And although this remains

John Gilbert, Mae Murray and Roy D'Arcy

Mae Murray and Tully Marshall

Roy D'Arcy, Mae Murray and John Gilbert

the film which won Mae Murray her best *acting* notices—and the *only* one for which she's widely remembered—the star could never, subsequently, find anything favorable to say about von Stroheim. For her, he would remain "that dirty Hun."

Of *The Merry Widow*'s male contingent, John Gilbert crossed over into superstardom, newcomer Roy D'Arcy soon found his scene-stealing evil much in demand, and Tully Marshall risked permanent identification as the silent screen's supreme dirty old man. For Erich von Stroheim, although the off-screen debacles of this picture and the previous *Greed* cost him his MGM contract, *The Merry Widow* marked the one and only unqualified box-office success of his career as a Hollywood director. In 1934, Ernst Lubitsch resurrected the *Widow* as a vehicle for the last reunion of Jeanette MacDonald and Maurice Chevalier, and a 1952 remake teamed a soprano-dubbed Lana Turner with Fernando Lamas. Both offered a wealth of Lehar music but little of the wild, hothouse glamour of von Stroheim's silent version.

John Gilbert and Mae Murray.

Anthony Jowitt and Gloria Swanson

THE COAST OF FOLLY

1925

CREDITS

A Paramount Picture. A Famous Players-Lasky Production. Produced and directed by Allan Dwan. Scenario by Forrest Halsey. Adapted by James Creelman from the novel by Coningsby Dawson. Photographed by George F. Webber. Seven reels.

CAST

Gloria Swanson (*Nadine Gathway/Joyce Gathway*); Anthony Jowitt (*Larry Fay*); Alec B. Francis (*Count de Tauro*); Dorothy Cumming (*Constance Fay*); Jed Prouty (*Cholly Knickerbocker*); Eugenie Besserer (*Nanny*); Arthur Housman (*Reporter*); Lawrence Gray (*Bather*); Charles Clary and Richard Arlen (*Bit Players*).

Gloria Swanson. The name alone conjures up a fabulous, bygone era of extravagant Hollywood glamour, elegant gowns and impassioned romantic dramas with titles like *Don't Change Your Husband* (1919), *The Affairs of Anatol* (1921), *Prodigal Daughters* (1923), *Manhandled* (1924) and *The Trespassser* (1929), her successful talkie debut. Swanson made more films after that, though not too many, including her dynamic comeback in 1950's *Sunset Boulevard*. But her major film career belonged to the Twenties, and in stories that naturally attracted more women ticket-buyers than men, since Gloria's appeal was more as clotheshorse than sex symbol. But she had a "face," with large, expressive eyes, and possessed a natural flair for comedy as well as drama. Tiny of figure, Swanson had a head somewhat large for her body, but clever costuming and considerate direction helped to mask those deficiencies.

Swanson enjoyed her role in 1925's *The Coast of Folly*, because it afforded her the opportunity to play two different roles, a young woman and her mother (whom she also portrayed briefly as a girl). Allan Dwan, who had been responsible for five previous Swanson vehicles (among them, *Zaza*, *A Society Scandal* and *Her Love*

Anthony Jowitt, Gloria Swanson, Richard Arlen and Alexander Gray

Story), directed. Years later, Dwan recalled, "It wasn't a blockbuster, but it was a good commercial picture."

The story is purest soap opera. It begins in 1905 with Gloria as Nadine Gathway (presumably about thirty), who shows her independence with her prig of a husband by walking out on both him and their young daughter, exchanging her stifling home-life for the pursuit of pleasure and wealth. Twenty years later, on the French Riviera, Nadine has become the Countess de Tauro (Gloria in age make-up that makes her look almost *elderly*) and is once again bored with a dull husband (Alec B. Francis). Meanwhile, back in the States, young Joyce Gathway (Swanson in natural, youthful make-up) risks losing her family inheritance because of an innocent friendship with a married man, Larry Fay (Anthony Jowitt). But Fay's wife Constance (Dorothy Cumming) suspects the worst, and she brings suit for alienation of affections. Learning of this incipient scandal, the Countess rallies to her daughter's defense, cleverly establishing a compromising situation against Constance so that she (the Countess) can "blackmail" her into withdrawing the lawsuit. Which she does. Following a divorce, Larry will be free to marry Joyce.

Dorothy Cumming and Gloria Swanson

Gloria Swanson

In her autobiography, *Swanson on Swanson*, the actress expressed satisfaction with this movie, because "for all the script's sentimentality, it gave me great opportunities to show my versatility." She admitted to having made the middle-aged countess a blend of novelist Elinor Glyn, actress Fannie Ward and her own mother, and she concluded, "I had not stretched so far in years, and the exertion gratified me."

Audiences probably enjoyed the pleasure of seeing their favorite glamour star in three different guises, but *The Coast of Folly*'s critics had a few reservations. *The New York Times* expressed appreciation of her make-up as the Countess, while reporting, "at times she exaggerates the walk of the elderly woman, making it appear rather that of a woman of eighty instead of fifty." (But was fifty considered "elderly" in 1925?) *Variety*'s reviewer was more succinct; "Miss Swanson as the old woman is very bad."

All seemed to agree, however, that Gloria Swanson was the main reason for attending this film. Of her leading men, the long-forgotten Anthony Jowitt made only a few other pictures in the mid-Twenties; small-part player Lawrence Gray soon went on to bigger roles, but never became a major star; and Richard Arlen, whose bit role fell victim to Paramount's cutting-room, enjoyed the lengthiest career of them all.

THE PHANTOM OF THE OPERA

1925

CREDITS

A Universal Picture. Produced by Carl Laemmle. Directed by Rupert Julian. Additional scenes directed by Edward Sedgwick. Screenplay by Raymond Schrock and Elliott J. Clawson. Based on the novel *Le Fantome de l'Opera* by Gaston Leroux. Titles by Tom Reed. Photographed by Virgil Miller, with sequences in Technicolor. Additional photography by Milton Bridenbecker and Charles J. Van Enger. Edited by Maurice Pivar. Art Direction by Charles D. Hall. Ten reels.

CAST

Lon Chaney (*Erik, the Phantom*); Mary Philbin (*Christine Daae*); Norman Kerry (*Raoul de Chagny*); Arthur Edmund Carewe (*Ledoux*); Gibson Gowland (*Simon Buquet*); John Sainpolis (*Philippe de Chagny*); Snitz Edwards (*Florine Papillon*); Virginia Pearson (*Carlotta*); Edith Yorke (*Mama Valerius*); Anton Vaverka (*Prompter*); Bernard Siegel (*Joseph Buquet*); Olive Ann Alcorn (*La Sorelli*); Cesare Gravina (*Manager*); George B. Williams (*Ricard*); Bruce Covington (*Moncharmin*); Edward Cecil (*Faust*); John Miljan (*Valentin*); Alexander Bevani (*Mephistopheles*); Grace Marvin (*Martha*); Ward Crane (*Count Ruboff*); Chester Conklin (*Orderly*); William Tryoler (*Director of Opera Orchestra*).

Of all Lon "Man-of-a-Thousand-Faces" Chaney's multitude of bizarre and grotesque characterizations for the silent screen (he made but one talkie, 1930's *The Unholy Three*, before his death that year), he's now best remembered for his classic impersonations of Quasimodo in *The Hunchback of Notre Dame* (1923) and Erik, the masked maniac who haunted the Paris Opera. This latter melodrama was adjudged by *Variety* critic "Skig" to be so horrific that he concluded, "It's impossible to believe there are a majority of picturegoers who prefer this revolting sort of a tale on the screen." Fortunately, for Universal Pictures, audiences *did* take to *The Phantom of the Opera*, for the company had expended nearly a million dollars (in 1925, a considerable sum) on the film. An appreciable portion of that went into the elaborate construction of a remarkably detailed reproduction of the opera house itself (known thereafter as "the Phantom set"), including secret passages, chambers and subcellars. Production costs also included a $50,000 expenditure on retakes, filmed by a different director and camera crew,

Lon Chaney and Mary Philbin

Lon Chaney

following the movie's disappointing reception at a San Francisco preview.

This oft-filmed melodrama derives from Gaston Leroux's 1910 novel, a wondrously bizarre thriller whose lurid plot complexities have been best approximated by the adaptation presently under discussion. Subsequent talkie remakes, released in 1943 (with Claude Rains as the Phantom), in 1962 (Herbert Lom) and 1982 (made-for-TV with Maximilian Schell) have tended to dissipate the story's thrill elements in favor of humor, sentimentality—and opera.

The 1925 *Phantom* centers on Christine Daae (Mary Philbin), a pretty young understudy at the Paris Opera whose voice appears to be the obsessive concern of a Svengali-like Phantom (Lon Chaney), whose ghostly but compelling voice issues from behind her dressing-room walls. Eventually they meet, and Christine witnesses a sinister, masked figure who exercises an uncanny power over her, forcing her to abandon her fiancé Raoul (Norman Kerry) in favor of both her career and her new mentor. The Phantom instigates strange "accidents" at the opera house, which enable Christine to succeed the leading soprano onstage in *Faust*. But when he realizes that Christine hasn't kept their agreement, and has continued to see Raoul, the Phantom kidnaps her and takes her to his secret apartment beneath the theatre. There she manages to remove his mask, recoiling in horror at the hideous sight beneath, and triggering a series of melodramatic incidents that eventually result in her rescue by Raoul and the Phantom's demise.

Apart from Chaney's self-styled, skull-like monster visage, which makes the celebrated unmasking scene the picture's highlight, this is not so much an actor's film as a director's vehicle. Director Rupert Julian cleverly arranges both Chaney and Mary Philbin to face the camera as she furtively slips off the mask so that *we* see the horror before *she* does. Philbin passes through the film looking attractive and suitably frightened, but Norman Kerry is wooden and uninvolved as her male counterpart. Director Julian fleshes out the melodrama with eerie atmosphere and a powerful visual sense, highlighted by such scenes as the Phantom's sudden Red Death appearance among the uneasy guests at a *bal masque* (filmed in Technicolor), and his subsequent appearance perched atop a gargoyle on the Opera's roof, where Christine is enjoying a secret rendezvous with Raoul. But another dramatic highlight, the exciting scene in which

Lon Chaney

the Phantom unlooses a giant chandelier on the opera's audience, seems abrupt and lacking in the suspense generated by Universal's 1943 remake.

Despite a mixed critical reception, *The Phantom of the Opera* proved so great a money-maker for the studio that, in 1929, it was re-released in a somewhat altered version, complete with talking sequences and operatic voices for the *Faust* scenes.

But it was Chaney's last film for Universal. A new contract with Metro-Goldwyn-Mayer would confine him to that studio for the remainder of his career.

Lon Chaney and Mary Philbin

THE EAGLE

1925

CREDITS

A United Artists Picture. An Art Finance Corp. Production. Presented by John W. Considine, Jr. Directed by Clarence Brown. Assistant Director: Charles Dorian. Screenplay by Hans Kraly. Titles by George Marion, Jr. Based on the story *Dubrovsky* by Alexander Pushkin. Photographed by George Barnes and J. Devereaux Jennings. Edited by Hal C. Kern. Art Direction by William Cameron Menzies. Costumes by Adrian. Technical Advisor: Michael Pleschkoff. Seven reels.

CAST

Rudolph Valentino (*Vladimir Dubrovsky*); Vilma Banky (*Mascha Troekouroff*); Louise Dresser (*Catherine II, the Czarina*); James Marcus (*Kyrilla Troekouroff*); George Nichols (*Judge*); Carrie Clark Ward (*Aunt Aurelia*); Michael Pleschkoff (*General Kuschka of the Cossack Guard*); Spottiswoode Aitken (*Dubrovsky's Father*); Gustav von Seyffertitz, Mario Carillo, Otto Hoffman, Eric Mayne, Jean De Briac, Albert Conti and Gary Cooper (*Bit Players*).

The Eagle was a veritable "comeback" film for Rudolph Valentino, the smouldering Latin Lover star whom Paramount had misused—and his pretentious designer-actress wife Natacha Rambova had misguided into performing—in such inappropriate and unpopular vehicles as *The Young Rajah* (1922) and *A Sainted Devil* (1924). He hadn't had an unqualified hit since 1922's *Blood and Sand*.

But *The Eagle*, directed for United Artists by Clarence Brown, benefitted enormously from a tongue-in-cheek approach by scenarist Hans Kraly (working from the unfinished Pushkin story *Dubrovsky*), who inspired Valentino to kid his own legend, as well as act the he-man lover that his more steadfast fans still preceived him to be. Brown had recently scored with a pair of excellent 1925 dramas, *Smouldering Fires* and *The Goose Woman*, and his stock was on the rise. *The Eagle* represented United Artists production chief Joseph Schenck's faith in the

Rudolph Valentino

director's work, considering that it was not only a costly production but also that a major star's career was at stake.

The Eagle is the tale of a Russian Robin Hood, with Valentino as Vladimir Dubrovsky, a young Cossack lieutenant who rescues a runaway carriage and its beautiful occupant (Vilma Banky), before returning a wandering horse to its titled owner, Catherine II (Louise Dresser, in a movie-stealing performance). The infamous Czarina wants to add Dubrovsky to her conquests, but he rejects her advances and, when he enlists her aid for his victimized father, she tries to have him arrested. At his parent's deathbed, the young man vows vengeance on Troekouroff (James Marcus), the vicious landowner responsible for the elder Dubrovsky's fall from wealth to poverty.

Rudolph Valentino, James Marcus and Vilma Banky

Rudolph Valentino and Louise Dresser

Assuming a bandit's disguise, young Dubrovsky becomes known locally as the Black Eagle. When his men capture Troekouroff's daughter Mascha, Dubrovsky recognizes her as the unknown beauty in the runaway carriage, and he lets her go. But he returns in the guise of a French tutor to infiltrate her father's house to both win her love and revenge himself on Troekouroff. Mascha is in on this deception all along and, since she reciprocates his love, willingly runs off with him to be married by a village priest. But their happiness is now cut short by the Czarina's guards, who capture Dubrovsky. However, his death sentence is commuted through the intervention of the Czarina's current favorite (Michael Pleschkoff), and the young lovers are free to enjoy their future together.

Expensively designed by the talented William Cameron Menzies and costumed by Adrian, *The Eagle* enjoyed that lucky combination of script, direction and performance that results in a motion picture of great entertainment value, as well as artistic quality. Deservedly, the movie was a tremendous hit, firmly reestablishing Valentino's once-solid status and probably best exemplifying the scope of his acting talents. This and his next vehicle for United Artists, *The Son of the Sheik* (1926), undoubtedly represent the best of the Italian-born actor's film legacy. Unfortunately, it also marked the end of his career. In August of 1926, Valentino suddenly fell ill and died of advanced peritonitis and attendant complications. He was only thirty-one.

Vilma Banky and Rudolph Valentino

TUMBLEWEEDS

1925

CREDITS

A United Artists Picture. A William S. Hart Production. Directed by King Baggot and (uncredited) William S. Hart. Screenplay by Hal G. Evarts and C. Gardner Sullivan, based on Evarts' *Saturday Evening Post* story. Photographed by Joseph August. Seven reels.

CAST

William S. Hart (*Don Carver*); Barbara Bedford (*Molly Lassiter*); Lucien Littlefield (*Kentucky Rose*); J. Gordon Russell (*Noll Lassiter*); Richard R. Neill (*Bill Freel*); Jack Murphy (*Bart Lassiter*); Lillian Leighton (*Mrs. Riley*); Gertrude Claire (*Old Woman*); George F. Marion (*Old Man*); Capt. T. E. Duncan (*Cavalry Major*); James Gordon (*Hinman, of the Box K Ranch*); Fred Gamble (*Hotel Proprietor*); Turner Savage (*Riley Boy*); Monte Collins (*Hicks*).

If it means anything today, the name of William S. Hart (1870–1946) is likely to conjure up the image of a stern-faced, narrow-eyed, middle-aged, two-gun hero of ancient Westerns. But, despite the fact that his prolific, eleven-year film career was almost exclusively confined to the Western milieu, Hart originally hailed from Newburgh, New York, Starting on the stage at nineteen, he found success early on as a Shakespearean actor, and also scored a hit as the villain Messala in the 1899 Broadway production of *Ben-Hur*. Hart's intense interest in the American West stemmed from his itinerant wanderings across the country as a teen-ager, and his initial portrayals of the Western hero took place in stage presentations of such classic stories as *The Squaw Man* and *The Virginian*.

Hart didn't make his first movie until 1914, when he was a mature forty-four, often directing or co-directing his own vehicles, initially under the aegis of producer Thomas H. Ince, and later for Paramount, in such popular titles as *Hell's Hinges* (1916), *Riddle Gawne* (1918) and *The Testing Block* (1920). His pictures never glorified the West; Hart insisted on absolute naturalism in

William S. Hart

Richard R. Neill, Barbara Bedford, William S. Hart and Jack Murphy

Richard R. Neill, Barbara Bedford and William S. Hart

plotting, setting and wardrobe. His eventual split with Paramount was the result of a refusal to compromise those ideals—in the light of his declining popularity—and adopt the showmanship of his slick, younger competitors in the genre like Buck Jones, Hoot Gibson and Ken Maynard.

Tumbleweeds, Hart's unplanned swan song, is an excellent motion picture centering on the opening of Oklahoma's Cherokee Strip to competing homesteaders in 1889. Its highlight, an exciting land-rush climax, was a masterpiece of sweeping direction, photography (often in striking silhouette) and editing. Filmed under an agreement with United Artists, *Tumbleweeds* cost Hart $300,000 to film and, in its final seven-reel cut, dissatisfied that distribution company, which wanted a *five*-reel movie. When Hart refused to cut the film, U.A. held up *Tumbleweeds'* release, thereby losing Hart some $500,000 in expected profits and ending in a bitter lawsuit between the two parties. Eventually, the actor-producer won $278,000 in damages, but the experience soured him on further filmmaking, despite *Tumbleweeds'* success. At fifty-five, he retired to his California ranch and rechanneled his creative drive into writing Western novels and an autobiography.

In 1939, *Tumbleweeds* was re-released by Astor Pictures, with sound effects, a musical score and—most notable of all—the addition of an eight-minute prologue in which Hart, filmed in a rugged outdoor setting, reminisced with his audience about the movie's historical background and his own past enjoyment as a Western performer. Finally, with a poignant farewell and a bow to the camera, Hart literally walked away into his private twilight.

THE UNCHASTENED WOMAN

1925

CREDITS

A Chadwick Picture. Directed by James Young. Scenario by Douglas Doty. Based on the play by Louis K. Anspacher. Photographed by William O'Connell. Seven reels.

CAST

Theda Bara (*Caroline Knollys*); Wyndham Standing (*Hubert Knollys*); Dale Fuller (*Hildegarde Sanbury*); John Miljan (*Lawrence Sanbury*); Harry Northrup (*Michael Krellin*); Eileen Percy (*Emily Madden*); Mayme Kelso (*Susan Ambie*).

There are many, it seems, who, upon recognizing the name Theda Bara, automatically associate her with the Twenties. Actually, Bara's major career belongs to the Teens, where she blazed magnificently for a few short years (1915–1919) and then virtually disappeared. As a more-or-less manufactured star, this saucer-eyed, exotic-looking and rather *zaftig* woman had emerged from the "extra" ranks when selected to portray the *femme fatale* heroine of *A Fool There Was* (1915) at the Fox studio. William Fox couldn't afford to cast an established star in the role, and so he put the twenty-five-year-old novice into the hands of studio coaches, make-up artists and publicists. This was not only to create the persona of a knock-'em-dead movie vampire, but also to make the public aware of a woman who, they'd have us believe, was born in the shadow of the Sphinx, out of wedlock to a French artist and his Arab mistress...and other such nonsense.

Although factual substantiation appears to have eluded most film historians, it seems most likely that Theda, as has often been reported, was born Theodosia Goodman in Cincinnati, Ohio, and that the "Theda" emerged from a contraction of her first name, while "Bara"" was a family surname. All of her other studio publicity appears to have been pure fabrication.

Theda Bara

Theda Bara and John Miljan

Theda Bara and Wyndham Standing

After *A Fool There Was* created an immediate sensation, Fox wasted no time cashing in on the film phenomenon by subsequently rushing his new star into one vehicle after another. In nearly all of these movies she played variations on the same unrepentant-mankiller theme, either in contemporary melodrama or as such

notorious ladies of history and/or literary legend as *Carmen* (1915), *The Eternal Sappho* (1916), *Camille* (1917), *Cleopatra* (1917), *Madame Du Barry* (1918) and *Salome* (1918). Having made forty-odd motion pictures in five years, it's no wonder that Theda Bara exhausted the public's fascination with her, becoming a victim of Fox's persistent type-casting of his biggest money-maker. For three years, Theda placed third (after Mary Pickford and Charlie Chaplin) at the box-office. In 1919, when Fox attempted to make her fans accept her as a simple Irish peasant girl in *Kathleen Mavourneen*, it was already too late. Much of her work received critical acclaim, and it's possible Theda Bara could eventually have become celebrated for her *acting*. Between 1914 and 1918, the actress's salary rose from $75 a week to $4,000, with the cost of her productions increasing commensurately. But by 1919 her vogue had considerably diminished. Suffering from tension and overwork, Bara suffered a nervous breakdown, and Fox allowed her contract to run out. She then left Hollywood and tried the stage.

In 1925, the screen's greatest vamp made a comeback, returning to films in *The Unchastened Woman* for the small independent Chadwick Pictures Corporation. Based on an old 1915 stage comedy-drama about marital transgression, it had been considered quite daring in those days. Not so in 1925, with Theda as a wife on the verge of announcing her pregnancy to her husband (Wyndham Standing) when she finds him in the arms of his secretary (Eileen Percy). Keeping mum about the baby, she takes off for Europe (leaving hubby with his doxy), has her child and becomes a notable fixture on the Continent. Eventually, she returns with a young architect (John Miljan) in tow as her protégé. By now, the husband is finally jealous, has tired of his secretary and feels repentant. But his independent-minded wife is initially unyielding. However, when she shows him their son, the child reunites them.

The Unchastened Woman, with Chadwick's limited publicity resources behind it, garnered little attention and wasn't successful. The following year, comedy producer Hal Roach persuaded Theda to kid her old vamp image in a two-reel farce entitled *Madame Mystery* (1926), in which she appeared with Oliver Hardy and James Finlayson, under the joint direction of Stan Laurel and Richard Wallace. But after that she retired from the screen to enjoy domestic life with her husband, movie director Charles Brabin.

Unfortunately, nearly all of Theda Bara's films are now lost to the ravages of fire and celluloid disintegration, but remnants of her legend live on sixty years after she left the screen. Such immortality deserves respect.

BEN-HUR

1925

Claire McDowell and Ramon Novarro

Francis X. Bushman, Ramon Novarro and May McAvoy

CREDITS

A Metro-Goldwyn-Mayer Picture. Produced by Louis B. Mayer and Irving Thalberg. Directed by Fred Niblo. Additional Direction by Ferdinand P. Earle. Second-Unit Director: B. Reeves Eason. Assistant Director: Charles Stallings. Scenario by Bess Meredyth and Carey Wilson. Titles by Katherine Hilliker and H. H. Caldwell. Adaptation by June Mathis. Based on the novel by General Lew Wallace. Photographed by Rene Guissart, Percy Hilburn, Karl Struss and Clyde De Vinna. Additional Photography by E. Burton Steene and George Meehan. Trick Photography by Paul Eagler. Nativity sequence filmed in Technicolor. Edited by Lloyd Nosler, assisted by Basil Wrangell, William Holmes, Harry Reynolds, Ben Lewis and (uncredited) Irving Thalberg. Sets by Cedric Gibbons, Horace Jackson and Arnold Gillespie. Artistic Effects by Ferdinand P. Earle. Costumes by Hermann J. Kaufmann. Traveling Mattes by Frank D. Williams. Musical Score by William Axt and David Mendoza. Production Manager: Harry Edington. Production Assistants: Silas Clegg, Alfred Raboch and William Wyler. Twelve reels.

CAST

Ramon Novarro (*Ben-Hur*); Francis X. Bushman (*Messala*); May McAvoy (*Esther*); Claire McDowell (*Mother of Hur*); Kathleen Key (*Tirzah*); Carmel Myers (*Iras*); Nigel de Brulier (*Simonides*); Mitchell Lewis (*Sheik Ilderim*); Leo White (*San Ballat*); Frank Currier (*Quintus Arrius*); Charles Belcher (*Balthasar*); Betty Bronson (*Mary*); Dale Fuller (*Amrah*); Winter Hall (*Joseph*); Myrna (Loy) Williams and Clark Gable (*Extras*).

Ben-Hur, a spectacular motion picture proposition in any era, has to date been filmed three times—first, in a condensed, primitive 1907 adaptation, directed by Sidney Olcott; then, Fred Niblo's 1925 version for MGM; and Metro's eleven-Oscar-winning 1969 remake, under the guidance of William Wyler, himself a production assistant on the Niblo version. Each film was costly, and all were immensely popular with the filmgoing public. But none had the problems attendant on the *Ben-Hur* of 1925.

A costly false-start saw *Ben-Hur* begin production in 1923 in Italy, under the seasoned direction of Charles Brabin, with the ruggedly handsome and popular George Walsh in the title role, and Gertrude Olmstead as his leading lady. But things did not go well on location and, after great expense was committed to sets, props and costumes, the initial completed footage was judged unusable. The April 1924 merger of Goldwyn Productions with Metro Pictures and Mayer Productions had resulted, of course, in the formation of Metro-Goldwyn-Mayer, with Irving Thalberg, the former "Boy Wonder" of Universal, now the supervisor of MGM production. Possessed of a tough head for business, Thalberg tightened the loose reins on this already-over-budget *Ben-Hur*, and halted production, secretly dispatching Fred Niblo and Ramon Novarro to Italy to replace, respectively, Brabin and Walsh, while Bess Meredyth and Carey Wilson took over scripting from June Mathis. Soon thereafter, *Ben-Hur* relocated to California, where the immense Antioch Coliseum set was constructed on a field near the studio. Italian locations had resulted in completion of only one-third of the movie—and at an expenditure of some two million dollars, during more than a year of filming.

The story opens in Jerusalem, then under the oppressive power of Imperial Rome. Ben-Hur (Roman Novarro), a Jewish prince of the house of Hur, enjoys a friendship with the Roman centurion Messala (Francis X. Bushman) that turns to enmity when the latter's incipient anti-Semitism surfaces. When a loosened tile falls from the house of Hur, killing a passing Roman general, Messala arrests the entire family to solidify himself with the governor. Ben-Hur is then sentenced to galley slavery; he later encounters Christ, Who refreshes the exhausted slave with water.

Ben-Hur saves the life of the ship commander Quintus Arrius (Frank Currier), who adopts the young man. He then finds popularity as a skilled charioteer. Ben-Hur and Messala meet again when they compete in a spectacular race in which the former triumphantly satisfies his need for revenge. In the company of Esther (McAvoy) and her father Simonides (Nigel de Brulier), Ben-Hur finds love and attains wealth.

Back in Jerusalem, the young man becomes a believer in the teachings of Jesus, Who heals the youth's mother and sister (Claire McDowell, Kathleen Key) of leprosy before being arrested. Ben-Hur attempts to raise an army to rescue Him, but is dissuaded by Christ, Who gently tells him that this is God's will. At the Crucifixion, Ben-Hur embraces Christianity.

Francis X. Bushman and Ramon Novarro

The movie's highlight, of course, is the exciting and spectacular chariot race—a still-impressive piece of footage that helps account for the film's great popularity, even in its somewhat abbreviated 1931 re-release, when a synchronized musical score and sound effects were added. *Ben-Hur* had cost MGM close to four million dollars (in 1925, an *enormous* outlay), but eventually the movie drew box-office returns of approximately nine million.

THE SEA BEAST

1926

John Barrymore

CREDITS

A Warner Bros. Picture. Directed by Millard Webb. Assistant Director: George Webster. Scenario by Bess Meredyth. Based on the novel *Moby Dick* by Herman Melville. Photographed by Byron Haskin and Frank Kesson. Ten reels.

CAST

John Barrymore (*Ahab Ceeley*); Dolores Costello (*Esther Harper*); George O'Hara (*Derek Ceeley*); Mike Donlin (*Flask*); Sam Baker (*Queequeeg*); George Burrell (*Perth*); Sam Allen (*Sea Captain*); Frank Nelson (*Stubbs*); Mathilde Comont (*Mula*); James Barrows (*Reverend Harper*); Vadim Uraneff (*Pip*); Sojin (*Fedallah*); Frank Hagney (*Daggoo*).

Herman Melville's mystical-symbolic 1851 novel *Moby Dick* detailed the dogged pursuit of a ferocious white whale by the vengeful Captain Ahab, whose leg the giant sea mammal had once bitten off. The story is told through the eyes of a young sailor named Ishmael, who signs aboard the doomed whaling ship *Pequod*, along with the bizarre harpooner Queequeeg. That chase takes the *Pequod* halfway around the earth before a climactic confrontation occurs between man and whale, resulting in the destruction of the ship and all aboard save Ishmael, who is rescued by another ship and, of course, lives to tell the tale.

Melville's classic somehow defied Hollywood filmmakers' efforts to turn it into a motion picture—until, in 1926, screenwriter Bess Meredyth, at the behest of Warner Bros., considerably altered the original to serve as a vehicle for John Barrymore that would also include a love interest! And so, Ahab (Barrymore) was now presented as a harpooner having not only a beautiful sweetheart called Esther (Dolores Costello, whom Barrymore would later marry), but also a rival for her affections in his half-brother Derek (George O'Hara). In this version, re-titled *The Sea Beast*, Ahab still loses that leg when, during a whaling expedition, the jealous Derek pushes Ahab overboard and he tangles with the vicious white whale Moby Dick. The one-legged, now-embittered Ahab tries to forget Esther (Derek convinces his brother she doesn't love him) by concentrating obsessively on the killing of Moby Dick. With the passage of time, Ahab becomes the captain of a whaler. Eventually,

Sojin, Sam Baker and John Barrymore

John Barrymore and Dolores Costello

John Barrymore

he destroys his nemesis and gets revenge on his brother in a fight. With his lust for vengeance satisfied, Ahab returns to New Bedford to settle down with the still-waiting Esther.

All of this romanticization of Melville was doubtless necessary for acceptance by a mid-Twenties movie audience, for his fans would never have accepted a romantic adventure film in which John Barrymore, then still cutting a highly attractive, matinee-idol figure at forty-three, might be bested by a giant whale. And even when the actor re-made the story in a 1931 talkie version (this time using the *Moby Dick* title), Ahab still had a love interest, as played by blond Joan Bennett. Not until John Huston's striking 1956 production would *Moby Dick* be filmed in anything like its original form.

During three weeks of location shooting on a whaling schooner near California's famed Catalina Island, John Barrymore worked hard to make up for the softening of Melville's book (he had originally objected to the love-interest changes) by doing his own stuntwork, battling the huge prop whale in the churning waters, and generally helping to make *The Sea Beast* as realistic a sea yarn as could be turned out, under the circumstances. A harrowing dramatic highlight was the scene in which Ahab's torn leg-stump must be cauterized by his fellow seamen. And the actor's make-up is occasionally as extraordinary here as his acting, turning him into an uncanny replica of his brother Lionel.

The Sea Beast opened to great and immediate success at the nation's box-offices, bringing the brothers Warner both more acclaim and profit than they had ever anticipated. In particular, Barrymore's performance brought out the most effusive of critical adjectives, and although there were some reservations about the movie's sluggish moments, few could find fault with the work of a charismatic actor in his late prime.

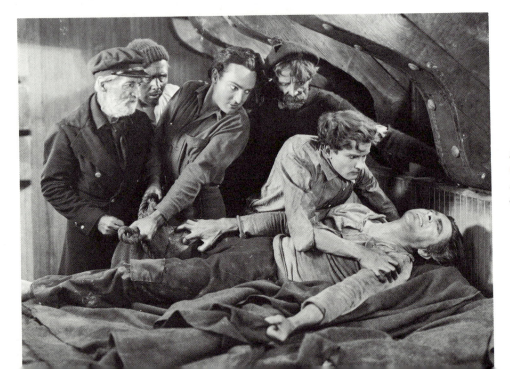

Sam Allen, Mike Donlin, George O'Hara, George Burrell, Frank Nelson and John Barrymore

ELLA CINDERS

1926

Lloyd Hughes and Colleen Moore

Colleen Moore

Vera Lewis, Colleen Moore and unidentified players

CREDITS

A First National Picture. A John McCormick Production. Directed by Alfred E. Green. Scenario by Frank Griffin and Mervyn LeRoy. Titles by George Marion, Jr. Based on the syndicated comic strip by William Conselman and Charles Plumb. Photographed by Arthur Martinelli. Edited by Robert J. Kern. Art Direction by E. J. Shulter. Seven reels.

CAST

Colleen Moore (*Ella Cinders*); Lloyd Hughes (*Waite Lifter*); Vera Lewis ("*Ma*" *Cinders*); Doris Baker (*Lotta Pill*); Emily Gerdes (*Prissy Pill*); Mike Donlin (*Film Studio Gateman*); Jed Prouty (*The Mayor*); Jack Duffy (*The Fire Chief*); Harry Allen (*The Photographer*); D'Arcy Corrigan (*The Editor*); Alfred E. Green (*The Director*); Harry Langdon (*Himself*); E. H. Calvert, Chief Yowlachie and Russell Hopton (*Bit Players*).

Colleen Moore was a well-born Michigander who began in films in 1917, aged seventeen, as the heroine of program pictures and Westerns. Later she became popular as a lively, jazz-age flapper at First National Pictures. Years before Hollywood ever heard of Louise Brooks, Moore made popular the feminine version of the Dutch-boy bob that also characterized child star Jackie Coogan, and which Brooks later modified—and is sometimes thought to have trademarked. Colleen Moore's movies are seldom seen and little-remembered today, which is a pity, because she was quite justifiably, next to Mary Pickford, one of the silent screen's highest paid and most popular stars. In fact, an industrial journal's 1926 poll of motion-picture theatre owners named her America's number one box-office attraction.

Many of Colleen Moore's best films were light romantic comedies produced by John McCormick, the first of her three husbands. Among these, 1926's *Ella Cinders* survives to delight audiences anew sixty years after it was first released, and most of the movie's charm is directly attributable to its delightful leading lady, cast as a small-town slavey who, like the fictional Cinderella, is victimized by a mean stepmother and selfish sisters, with whom she lives and to whom she must act as servant. In *Ella Cinders*, salvation comes through both the unexpected winning of a phony movie contest and the love of a handsome football-champ-turned-iceman (Lloyd Hughes), who permits her departure for Hollywood, but is waiting for her when she changes her mind about movie stardom.

The picture is at its best when Ella is involved in some of the clever gags devised by co-scenarist Mervyn LeRoy at a time when that director-to-be was a top-notch "comedy construction specialist." Thus, Ella's hilarious session with a portrait photographer and her various *faux pas* on the sets of a motion picture studio, where she utterly devastates a day's shooting, provide classic examples of silent-screen farce of the more gentle variety.

With a popular comic strip as its source material, *Ella Cinders* offered Colleen Moore one of her best vehicles and, understandably, became a tremendous box-office hit. Its director, Alfred E. Green, who had already teamed with Moore on *Irene* (1926), also appeared on-camera as a director in the film's Hollywood-studio sequence, as did (to delightful effect) the popular comedian Harry Langdon, in an unbilled cameo. *Ella Cinders* remains truly a vintage silent comedy.

IT'S THE OLD ARMY GAME

1926

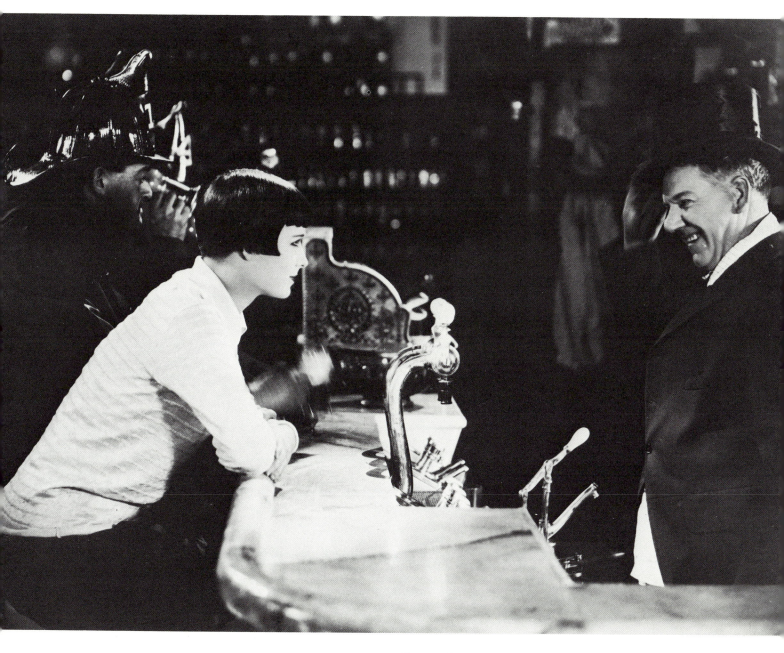

Louise Brooks and W.C. Fields

CREDITS

A Paramount Picture. A Famous Players-Lasky Production. Produced by Adolph Zukor and Jesse L. Lasky. Directed by Edward Sutherland. Story by Joseph P. McEvoy and William Le Baron. Scenario by Tom J. Geraghty. Titles by Ralph Spence. Photographed by Alvin Wyckoff. Edited by Tom J. Geraghty. Seven reels.

CAST

W. C. Fields (*Elmer Prettywillie*); Louise Brooks (*Marilyn Sheridan*); Blanche Ring (*Tessie Gilch*); William Gaxton (*William Parker*); Mary Foy (*Sarah Pancoast*); Mickey Bennett (*Mickey*); Josephine Dunn and Jack Luden (*Society Bathers*); George Currie (*Artist*).

W. C. Fields, that bulb-nosed misogynist remembered for his nasal, inimitably-cadenced speech patterns, didn't enter silent films until in his forties, after years in the vaudeville theatres. Initially he was an eccentric stage juggler before becoming an eccentric comedian, and was featured in the *Follies* of that flamboyant showman Florenz Ziegfeld.

In the Twenties, W. C. Fields was an accomplished stage clown entering the competitive ranks of film, where he learned to adapt his offbeat style to the pantomime shadow-world then ruled by Chaplin, Keaton and Lloyd. Fields began in Manhattan-filmed short comedies, played a cameo role in the Marion Davies costume drama *Janice Meredith* (1924) and graduated to leading roles with *Sally of the Sawdust* (1925). Today, Fields is revered as one of the unique purveyors of classic screen humor, a reputation largely gained from several inspired performances of the early Forties (especially *My Little Chickadee* and *The Bank Dick*), a period when his popularity had broadened through the medium of radio.

In *It's The Old Army Game*, Fields headlined a story loosely patched together from some of his old vaudeville and revue skits, especially those centering around a drugstore and a picnicking family. Unfortunately, this movie lacks sufficient faith in the comic talents of its nominal star, for it veers away to encompass a none-too-exciting sideline romance that develops between druggist Fields's vivacious young assistant (played by the charismatic starlet Louise Brooks) and a traveling con artist (stage actor William Gaxton, bidding unsuccessfully for a screen career).

Louise Brooks

The film's opening sequence seems an oddly extended "introduction" that makes little sense. In the early morning hours a strange, grimly determined woman races her car against a train, risking her life to cross its path. Reaching Fields's drugstore, she aggressively rings his night bell, rousing him from bed so that she can purchase a two-cent stamp (which she neglects to pay for) to mail a lettter. In so doing, she inadvertently sets off a fire alarm, thus bringing firemen to the drugstore in vain. After which a fire *does* break out in the store—in a cigar box! But why continue? None of the "plot" makes any sense, although much of it gives Fields opportunities to do his brand of comedy. And there are a few good laughs to be had from his trying to douse that cigar-box fire, as well as devastating a millionaire's lawn amid an impromptu picnic outing with his family.

It's The Old Army Game (a negligible title) was filmed both at Paramount's Astoria facilities and on location in Florida's Palm Beach, but it hardly seems to have been worth all the trouble. Louise Brooks recalls that director Edward Sutherland (who subsequently became her husband) and his cast were a uniformly party-loving group, perhaps too much so for the good of the picture.

Variety's critic "Fred." applauded W. C. Fields's efforts at utilizing "nearly every gag he ever saw or heard of." But he reserved his real praise for Louise Brooks, whom he said "photographs like a million dollars." And he concluded, "This girl is going to land right at the top in the picture racket."

But, of course, it would be Fields who would flourish with talking pictures, while Brooks (as she later admitted, through every fault of her own) would rapidly decline.

Blanche Ring, Mary Foy, Mickey Bennett and W.C. Fields

THE TEMPTRESS

1926

CREDITS

A Metro-Goldwyn-Mayer Picture. A Cosmopolitan Production. Directed by Fred Niblo and (uncredited) Mauritz Stiller. Assistant Director: Bruce Humberstone. Scenario by Dorothy Farnum. Titles by Marian Ainslee. Based on Vicente Blasco-Ibanez' novel *La Tierra de Todos* and its English translation by Leo Ongley, *The Temptress*. Photographed by Gaetano ("Tony") Gaudio and William Daniels. Edited by Lloyd Nosler. Art Direction by Cedric Gibbons and James Basevi. Costumes by Andre-ani and Max Ree. Nine reels.

CAST

Greta Garbo (*Elena*); Antonio Moreno (*Robledo*); Roy D'Arcy (*Mano Duros*); Marc MacDermott (*Fontenoy*); Lionel Barrymore (*Canterac*); Virginia Brown Faire (*Celinda*); Armand Kaliz (*Torre Blanca*); Alys Murrell (*Josephine*); Robert Anderson (*Pirovani*); Francis McDonald (*Timoteo*); Hector V. Sarno (*Rojas*); Inez Gomez (*Sebastiana*); Steve Clemento (*Salvadore*); Roy Coulson (*Trinidad*).

MGM's glamorous Swedish import Greta Garbo had made so favorable an impression with her American debut in *The Torrent* (1926), based on a Blasco-Ibanez story, that the studio wasted no time casting her in a follow-up vehicle, *The Temptress*, also adapted from a work of the popular Spanish novelist. This time, the twenty-year-old actress was happy to know that her compatriot mentor, Mauritz Stiller, with whom she had made *Gosta Berling's Saga* (1924), would direct her. But ten days into production, Stiller was abruptly fired from the picture, apparently because his undisciplined methods, temperament and awkwardness with the English language were deemed unsuitable to a major Hollywood studio. And after a series of upsetting experiences with another autocratic European-born director, Erich von Stroheim, Metro was not about to contend again with the sort of problems encountered with *Greed* and *The Merry Widow*.

Greta Garbo

And so *The Temptress* resumed shooting under the helm of Fred Niblo, a director probably less sensitive to Garbo's personal insecurities, but more capable of giving the studio the movie they wanted. But many stills survive to reflect the original Stiller footage, noticeable by the inclusion of actor H. B. Warner (not in the finished film) and the fact that male lead Antonio Moreno is shown minus his trademark mustache (Stiller had fought with the actor, insisting that he be clean-shaven for this picture).

The Temptress, of course, owes most of its success to the magic of Garbo. Few actresses of her era could sustain the thesis of the movie's title so convincingly and yet with such passive allure. For the most part, Garbo's Elena is a

heroine more used by than using of the men she encounters. For her, men fight, kill and commit suicide. And Garbo persuades her audience to accept and believe it all.

From a loveless Paris marriage to a husband who permits her to be the mistress of another, this Circe of the Twenties finds true-love-at-first-sight at a costume ball, where she first encounters a visiting engineer from the Argentine, Robledo (Moreno). But he soon learns of her previous male entanglements and wisely decides he'd be better off far away from her. A romantic and highly unlikely plot takes him back to South America, where Elena and her husband (Armand Kaliz) soon join him to avoid a scandal in Paris. She soon has every man on

Armand Kaliz, Lionel Barrymore, Inez Gomez, Greta Garbo, Robert Anderson and Francis McDonald

Robledo's dam-building project fascinated with her. Subsequently, Elena's husband is killed, Robledo is forced to engage in a bullwhip duel over her with a local outlaw (Roy D'Arcy), and both a murder and the sabotaging of the dam are also blamed on her before she's finally packed off to Paris.

At this point, the narrative suddenly skips ahead six years and we're back in France with Robledo, who's there on a vacation with his "fiancée" Celinda (Virginia Brown Faire). Since this was the same girl who was after him six years earlier—when Elena was still on the scene—we are led to assume that Celinda still isn't a very exciting bridal prospect! And who should turn up to catch Robledo's eye but Elena, now a drink-sodden woman of the boulevards. Robledo tries to renew their acquaintance, but Elena appears not to recognize him at all, and the best he can do is buy her a drink, stuff money in her purse and leave her to fate—and the bottle.

After moving through most of *The Temptress* as a beautiful clotheshorse seemingly unable to control her devastating effect on the male sex, Garbo's fascinating Elena, in the movie's tragic final scenes, offers an utterly unforgettable portrait of hopeless degradation, dispelling any possible doubts as to the depths of her innate talents as an actress.

Greta Garbo and Antonio Moreno

EXIT SMILING

1926

Beatrice Lillie and Jack Pickford

Beatrice Lillie and Doris Lloyd

CREDITS

A Metro-Goldwyn-Mayer Picture. Directed by Sam Taylor. Scenario by Sam Taylor and Tim Whelan. Titles by Joe Farnham. Based on a story by Marc Connelly. Photographed by Andrew Barlatier. Edited by Daniel J. Gray. Sets by Cedric Gibbons and Frederic Hope. Costumes by Andre-ani. Seven reels.

CAST

Beatrice Lillie (*Violet*); Jack Pickford (*Jimmy Marsh*); Doris Lloyd (*Olga*); DeWitt Jennings (*Orlando Wainwright*); D'Arcy Corrigan (*Macomber*); Franklin Pangborn (*Cecil Lovelace*); Harry Myers (*Jesse Watson*); Carl Richards (*Dave*); Tenen Holtz (*Tod Powell*); William Gillespie (*Jack Hastings*); Louise Lorraine (*Phyllis Tichnor*).

Beatrice Lillie's 1926 American film debut followed a noteworthy success as the star comedienne of Andrew Charlot's stage revues from Britain, and although cinema audiences could not yet enjoy the pleasure of her unique voice and piquant delivery, the visual benefits of Lillie's pantomimic skills and sly, inventive wit lent themselves well to the silent screen.

MGM was careful to tailor *Exit Smiling* to Lillie's somewhat bizarre talents, engaging tried and true comedy experts to provide the showcase for her movie bow, with Sam Taylor, Harold Lloyd's favorite director, co-authoring the scenario with another Lloyd alumnus, Tim Whelan. Working from an original story by playwright Marc Connelly (*Merton of the Movies*), Taylor and Whelan had Bea Lillie be Violet, the all-purpose drudge of Orlando Wainwright's traveling repertory company. In that capacity, she also doubles as private maid to Olga (the underappreciated Doris Lloyd), the troupe's somewhat alcohol-prone leading lady. Violet is also a would-be actress, and eventually gets to appear onstage, attired in

Doris Lloyd, Jack Pickford, Beatrice Lillie and DeWitt Jennings

male drag, boots and mustache, understudying the villain of the Wainwright company's current bill, a melodrama entitled *Flaming Women*.

The plot complications center on Jimmy Marsh (played by Jack Pickford, Mary's less-celebrated brother), a small-town bank teller framed on a false forgery charge by a rival for the affections of the bank president's daughter Phyllis (Louise Lorraine). Discharged from his job, Jimmy joins the Wainwright troupe (as stagehand and under-study), through the intervention of Violet, who mistakenly fancies he's taken a shine to her. This one-sided "ro-mance" provides one of the movie's central—and most sympathetic—themes, and, because of Bea Lillie's roguish charm, it comes as a major letdown when the denouement sees a vindicated Jimmy leaving the troupe—and Violet—for his old love Phyllis.

Lillie and Pickford share equal billing in *Exit Smiling*, which is deceptive, because it's the English comedienne's film all the way, providing ample proof of the talent (for both comedy and pathos) that made her a unique star

and kept her on top for years to come. Unfortunately, for cinema audiences, the *stage* was to be her chief medium, with her motion picture appearances few and far be-tween. And, aside from *Exit Smiling*, perhaps only the 1945 *On Approval* made adequate celluloid use of her clever skills.

As for Jack Pickford, he starred in only one more picture, 1928's minor underworld melodrama *Gang War*, and finished his short life in the pursuit of pleasure and alcohol, dying at thirty-seven in 1933.

Lois Wilson, Warner Baxter, Hale Hamilton and Neil Hamilton

THE GREAT GATSBY

1926

CREDITS

A Paramount Picture. Presented by Adolph Zukor and Jesse L. Lasky. Produced and Directed by Herbert Brenon. Screenplay by Becky Gardiner. Adaptation by Elizabeth Meehan. Based on the novel by F. Scott Fitzgerald. Photographed by Leo Tover. Eight reels.

CAST

Warner Baxter (*Jay Gatsby*); Lois Wilson (*Daisy Buchanan*); Neil Hamilton (*Nick Carraway*); Georgia Hale (*Myrtle Wilson*); William Powell (*George Wilson*); Hale Hamilton (*Tom Buchanan*); George Nash (*Charles Wolf*); Carmelita Geraghty (*Jordan Baker*); Eric Blore (*Lord Digby*); "Gunboat" Smith (*Bert*); Claire Whitney (*Catherine*).

F. Scott Fitzgerald's 1925 novel has, to date, been filmed three times: first, this silent 1926 version with Warner Baxter and Lois Wilson; then, after a twenty-three-year gap, its first sound adaptation starring Alan Ladd and Betty Field in 1949; and, most recently—with the addition of color—the expensive Robert Redford-Mia Farrow offering of 1974. None has proved an unqualified success; there has always been some undefinable something about the Fitzgerald book that defies filming. Perhaps it's the complexity of his literary characters, a certain mystic quality that continues to challenge students in their interpretation of the novel. Certainly, none of the actors attempting to portray either Jay Gatsby or Daisy Buchanan has managed to satisfy critics and audiences

William Powell

Warner Baxter and George Nash

Lois Wilson and Warner Baxter

with any approximation of unanimity.

Unfortunately, Herbert Brenon's 1926 motion picture is the only missing one of the lot, and thus currently unavailable for reevaluation (unless rumors of an existing print behind the Iron Curtain eventually prove valid). Brenon's version was also the most successful of the three, which isn't surprising in light of his then-exalted position as the director of *Peter Pan* (1924), *A Kiss for Cinderella* (1925) and *Beau Geste* (1926).

The Fitzgerald story is both structurally simple and psychologically complex. Gatsby (Warner Baxter) is a young Army officer of ordinary background who falls for Daisy Fay (Lois Wilson), a Long Island society deb with whom he exchanges declarations of eternal love before going off to the Great War. Gatsby determines to raise himself to her social position, but nine years pass before he reappears on the scene, now in posession of mysterious wealth and a Long Island estate. By this time, Daisy is the wife of well-born but dissolute Tom Buchanan (Hale Hamilton), who nevertheless maintains a mistress named Myrtle Wilson (Georgia Hale), the faithless wife of a garage-owner (William Powell). When her husband calls Gatsby a bootlegger and accuses him of having an affair with his wife, Daisy runs away with Gatsby. But their car strikes and kills the distraught Myrtle, and her husband retaliates by fatally shooting Gatsby.

Admittedly, both Daisy and the enigmatic Gatsby are difficult roles for actors to characterize successfully, and the best word *The New York Times* could find for the performances of Warner Baxter and Lois Wilson was "conscientious." William Powell, then establishing a solid reputation as a young character actor, won praise for his "unerring portrayal."

Although the silent *Gatsby* remains unavailable to American film scholars, Lois Wilson recalls its production as "a wonderful experience." And, perhaps, gathering dust in some Soviet film archive...

OLD IRONSIDES
(Sons of the Sea)

1926

Charles Farrell

CREDITS

A Paramount Picture. A Famous Players-Lasky Production. Presented by Adolph Zukor and Jesse L. Lasky. Production supervised by B. P. Schulberg. Directed by James Cruze. Assistant Director: Harold Schwartz. Scenario by Dorothy Arzner, Walter Woods and Harry Carr. Based on a story by Laurence Stallings. Titles by Rupert Hughes. Photographed by Alfred Gilks and Charles Boyle. Special Effects by Roy Pomeroy. Score by Hugo Riesenfeld. Eight reels.

CAST

Charles Farrell (*The Boy/The Commodore*); Esther Ralston (*The Girl/Esther*); Wallace Beery (*The Bo'sn*); George Bancroft (*The Gunner*); Charles Hill Mailes (*Commodore Preble*); Johnny Walker (*Lt. Stephen Decatur*); Eddie Fetherston (*Lt. Richard Somers*); George Godfrey (*Cook*); Guy Oliver (*First Mate*); Fred Kohler (*Second Mate*); Nick De Ruiz (*The Bashaw*); Mitchell Lewis (*Pirate Chief*); Edgar "Blue" Washington (*Negro*); Boris Karloff (*A Saracen guard*); Effie Ellsler (*Esther's Mother*); William Conklin (*Esther's Father*); Duke Kahanamoku (*Pirate Captain*); Spec O'Donnell (*Cabin Boy*); Tetsu Komai (*Pirate*); Jack Herrick (*Sailor*); Gary Cooper, Richard Arlen, William Bakewell and Dick Alexander (*Extras*).

Launched in 1797 and nicknamed "Old Ironsides," the frigate *Constitution* is probably the most famous vessel in the history of the United States Navy. Her participation in the Tripolitan War of 1800–15, instituted when the States rebelled against continuing to pay tribute as protection against pirate raids in the waters of the North African Barbary States, inspired the original story by Laurence Stallings on which this patriotic sea epic is based.

In a 1980 symposium of silent stars gathered at the Academy of Motion Picture Arts and Sciences, Esther Ralston named 1926's *Old Ironsides* as her favorite film, "because my people came over on the Mayflower, and they fought in the Revolutionary War, the Civil War, both World Wars and Vietnam. I think because *Old Ironsides* is history—American history—that it means more to me than any other of my pictures."

Old Ironsides, of course, is based on American history, but with the usual Hollywood augmentation of "love interest" and the deployment of dramatic license which most audiences expect in a good historical-adventure movie. All of which is inherent in the scenario devised from Stallings's story by future-director Dorothy Arzner, Walter Woods and Harry Carr. Famous Players-Lasky thought enough of the project to expend somewhere between $1,500,000 and a rumored $2,400,000 on its production, incorporating extensive outdoor shooting on full-scale reproductions of the *Constitution*, the frigate *Philadelphia* and the merchant barque *Esther* (on which much of the movie's action takes place). An enormous cast of extras (including the pre-stardom Gary Cooper and Richard Arlen) manned those ships as sailors and pirates. In 1926–27, *Old Ironsides*' scale and scope impressed the public as much as the press, especially in those theatres equipped to show it in the Magnascope process. This enabled projectionists to enlarge the screen to double its ordinary size for the marine sequences—an exciting innovation anticipating the wide-screen Cinerama projection of *Windjammer* in 1958.

Old Ironsides made a major star of handsome, stalwart twenty-one-year-old Charles Farrell, who soon afterward was cast opposite Janet Gaynor in the 1927 classic *Seventh Heaven*. That film would launch them as the top romantic team of the late silent–early talkie era.

In *Old Ironsides*, Farrell portrays the young hero, a naïve, New England country lad who leaves home lured by a poster promising adventure at sea. In the sailing capital of New Bedford, he's bamboozled by a clever but jovial bo'sn (Wallace Beery), through whose trickery both the boy and a gunner (George Bancroft) are shanghaied aboard the merchant vessel *Esther*, bound for Italy. Also aboard is the beautiful daughter (Esther Ralston) of the craft's owner, en route to join her father in Europe.

In an episodic narrative, the green farm boy fast becomes ship-shape, while he and the young lady fall hopelessly in love, embracing at the least likely moments, at one time threatening to capsize the ship when, in rough waters, he relinquishes the wheel for her kiss. But romance takes a back-seat to action when the *Esther* is captured by pirates. The male survivors are sold into slavery, while the girl is held aside as a prize for the Sultan. Meanwhile, the *Philadelphia* pursues a pirate ship into the harbor of Tripoli, but runs aground and is captured. And finally, it's "Old Ironsides" to the rescue! The *Constitution* sails onto the scene with guns ablaze,

Esther Ralston and Charles Farrell

sinking the pirate frigate and taking the fort. Hero and heroine are reunited, and the film's character-lead (Beery) is battle-scarred but still smiling at the fadeout.

All of this is directed with amazing coordination by James Cruze, whose reputation today hangs mainly on *The Covered Wagon*, that landmark Western epic he directed for Paramount in 1923. But *Old Ironsides* surely seems deserving of equal respect for its meticulous attention to maritime detail, with only the slightest recourse to any use of miniatures. And Cruze's direction of a huge cast is deceptively smooth, from the relatively inexperienced Charles Farrell to "comedy relief" character actors Beery and Bancroft and, as the *Esther*'s amusingly gruff black cook, real-life heavyweight champ George Godfrey in his movie debut. Some sixty years later, *Old Ironsides*, aside from the silence of its performers, seems scarcely dated at all.

Charles Farrell and Wallace Beery

TELL IT TO THE MARINES

1926

CREDITS

A Metro-Goldwyn-Mayer Picture. Directed by George Hill. Scenario by E. Richard Schayer. Titles by Joe Farnham. Photographed by Ira Morgan. Edited by Blanche Sewell. Sets by Cedric Gibbons and Arnold Gillespie. Musical score by William Axt. Nine reels.

CAST

Lon Chaney (*Sergeant O'Hara*); William Haines (*George "Skeet" Burns*); Eleanor Boardman (*Norma Dale*); Eddie Gribbon (*Corporal Madden*); Carmel Myers (*Zaya*); Warner Oland (*Chinese Bandit Leader*); Mitchell Lewis (*Native*); Frank Currier (*General Wilcox*); Maurice Kains (*Harry*).

Eleanor Boardman and Lon Chaney

Lon Chaney, Hollywood's foremost character actor of the Twenties, specialized in roles of a sinister, bizarre or gruesome nature, and seldom appeared without resort to unusual make-ups and/or physical hindrances. A distinctive exception was *Tell It to the Marines*, in which he portrayed a tough, no-nonsense sergeant with a minimum of greasepaint. What his public saw was a relatively rare public exposure of the actor's own homely features. In fact, the film's script plays off the character's so-called "ugliness," and Chaney appears to have gone along with the gimmick willingly.

Tell It to the Marines gives Chaney top billing, but the movie really belongs to William Haines, a personable actor whose popular forte was the portrayal of engagingly brash and cocky young men, manifesting the kind of appeal that thirty years later would adhere to Jack Lemmon.

Working from an excellent, if episodic and somewhat sprawling, original scenario by E. Richard Schayer, director George Hill (later to win acclaim for *The Big House* and *Min and Bill*) draws characterizations of well-observed humor and unglamorous recognizability from his star troika of Haines, Chaney and—the girl they both covet—the charming Eleanor Boardman.

William Haines and Lon Chaney

Lon Chaney, William Haines and Eddie Gribbon.

Tell It to the Marines begins on an "up" note as wiseguy recruit George "Skeet" Burns tries to put one over on the Marine Corps by having them finance his train trip from Kansas City to San Diego—and then splits for Tijuana, Mexico. But his plan backfires when his gambling money runs out, and he finds himself trying to wisecrack his way through basic training, under the unrelenting tutelage of O'Hara (Chaney), a sergeant for whom Skeet can do no right. When the lad makes a heavy play for Navy nurse Norma Dale (Boardman), a young woman O'Hara feels protective toward, he gets into hot water and lands in the brig. Incident piles episodically on incident, and Skeeet, the nervy misfit, slowly begins to adjust to the discipline of military life. Finally winning the heart of Norma, he bungles that relationship when, stationed temporarily in the Philippines, he's distracted by the obvious charms of Zaya (Carmel Myers), a "native" girl. After that episode, the movie gets steadily more serious, with Skeet and the Marines rescuing whites from bandits in China. Eventually, mature and responsible, Skeet makes peace with Norma and wins her hand. The movie ends as he pays a nostalgic visit to O'Hara, who's busy haranguing a gaggle of raw recruits.

Tell It to the Marines runs a bit long for its own good, and the serious themes of its later third seem out of kilter with the film's rambunctious early scenes. But its overall entertainment value pleased the moviegoers of 1926–27, making it one of that season's most popular attractions.

William Haines and Eleanor Boardman

William Haines and Carmel Myers

Lon Chaney and William Haines

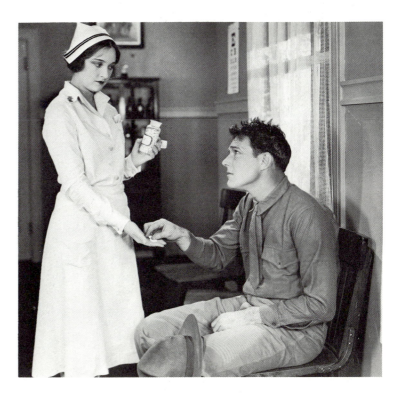

Eleanor Boardman and William Haines

SLIPPING WIVES

Stan Laurel, Priscilla Dean, Herbert Rawlinson and Oliver Hardy

1927

CREDITS

A Pathé Picture. Produced by Hal Roach. Supervised by F. Richard Jones. Directed by Fred L. Guiol. Directorial assistance by Lewis R. Foster. Story by Hal Roach. Titles by H. M. Walker. Photographed by George Stevens. Edited by Richard Currier. Costumes by Will Lambert. Two reels.

CAST

Priscilla Dean (*The Wife*); Herbert Rawlinson (*Leon, the Artist Husband*); Stan Laurel (*Ferdinand Flamingo, the Delivery Man*); Oliver Hardy (*Jarvis, the Butler*); Albert Conti (*The Hon. Winchester Squirtz*).

Stan Laurel and Oliver Hardy are today revered as the screen's master duo of screen comedy, quite outdistanc-

ing the teamwork of such past-favorite combos as Abbott and Costello, Martin and Lewis, and Wheeler and Woolsey. But in their heyday, Laurel and Hardy went unlauded by the film critics, and were quite taken for granted by the public. In the Fifties and Sixties, television brought them a whole new audience, as did producer Robert Youngson, with compilation films like *The Golden Age of Comedy* (1957), *Days of Thrills and Laughter* (1961) and *Laurel and Hardy's Laughing 20's* (1965).

The slightly-built Scotland-born Laurel was a music-hall comedian and Charles Chaplin's understudy with the Fred Karno Company during that troupe's first American vaudeville tour in 1910. Later, Laurel worked up a Chaplin impersonation, with which he toured U.S. vaudeville houses as Charlie's newly popular gentleman-tramp.

The more solidly constructed Hardy hailed from a good Georgia family, and began his performing career as

Oliver Hardy, Stan Laurel, Priscilla Dean and Herbert Rawlinson

a boy soprano with Coburn's Minstrels at the age of eight. Years later, while at the University of Georgia, disinterest caused him to abandon the study of law for the growing motion-picture industry, and he opened a film theatre in his hometown of Milledgeville, which he operated for three years. In 1913, hoping to turn his fun-loving extroversion into a profession, Hardy relocated to Jacksonville, Florida, where he succeeded in finding movie work as an actor with the Lubin Company.

Laurel and Hardy first worked together—but not as a team—in the 1917 two-reel comedy, *Lucky Dog*. Hardy was the star, with Laurel supporting him in the role of a masked bandit. Nine years would pass before the men worked together again, when both were placed under contract by Hal Roach. Despite their fame as a comedy team, Stan Laurel made 76 films without Hardy between 1916 and 1928, and Hardy filmed a whopping 214 movies without Laurel from 1914 to 1950.

In 1926 and 1927, their "formative" years with the

Roach Company, Laurel and Hardy (then, respectively, thirty-seven and thirty-five years of age) were not yet starred as a team. Instead, they acted as part of a comedy *ensemble*, typified by *Slipping Wives*, a two-reeler photographed by future-director George Stevens and starring Priscilla Dean, a once-popular leading lady of serials and melodramas whose career was on the wane. The movie's plot is that standard about a neglected wife's efforts to arouse her husband's jealousy by carrying on a flirtation. Here, her "dalliance" is with their handyman (Laurel), which leads to the expected confusions, frenetic chase scenes and bedroom titillations. For Laurel and Hardy, the emphasis is on pantomime. And, while no particular "teamwork" was planned for them in the writing of *Slipping Wives*, one notes a natural affinity in their performances. Together, the team made a total of 105 movies, mostly two-reelers. In 1935, under the title *The Fixer Uppers*, Stan and Ollie remade *Slipping Wives*, with their original roles enlarged.

THE KID BROTHER

1927

CREDITS

A Paramount Picture. A Harold Lloyd Corp. Production. Presented by Adolph Zukor and Jesse L. Lasky. Directed by Ted Wilde and (uncredited) J. A. Howe and Lewis Milestone. Assistant Director: Gaylord Lloyd. Story by John Grey, Ted Wilde and Tom Crizer. Scenario by John Grey, Lex Neal and Howard Green. Photographed by Walter Lundin and Henry N. Kohler. Edited by Allen McNeil. Art Direction by Liell K. Vedder. Technical Director: William MacDonald. Eight reels.

CAST

Harold Lloyd (*Harold Hickory*); Jobyna Ralston (*Mary Powers*); Walter James (*Jim Hickory*); Leo Willis (*Leo Hickory*); Olin Francis (*Olin Hickory*); Constantine Romanoff (*Sandoni*); Eddie Boland (*"Flash" Farrell*); Frank Lanning (*Sam Hooper*); Ralph Yearsley (*Hank Hooper*).

Harold Lloyd entered films as an extra in 1912, at the age of nineteen. It was his friendship with a fellow extra named Hal Roach that helped Lloyd graduate into leads in one-reel comedies two years later, when Roach inherited some money and began to produce his own pictures. In 1916–17, Lloyd starred as a character named "Lonesome Luke" in some one hundred popular, action-oriented comedy shorts for Roach. At first, these were styled after Charlie Chaplin's, but Lloyd later adopted such recognizable appurtenances as a pair of large, horn-rimmed spectacles and a straw hat. Like Chaplin, Lloyd remained in short films throughout the Teens, making his feature-film debut in 1921, the same year Chaplin turned out his first full-length movie in *The Kid*. But while Chaplin now began to take more and more pains with each film (producing only three long films and three short ones during the entire decade), Harold Lloyd starred in ten shorts and twelve features during the Twenties, a period during which he was without equal as America's favorite film comedian.

Today, Lloyd has long been eclipsed in nostalgia-popularity by Chaplin, Buster Keaton and the team of Laurel and Hardy. The availability of their films has much to do with this favoritism, for Lloyd's films, of which he retained the negatives, were long unseen, while the comedies of his contemporaries were revived and recycled. Rediscovery of his work was helped by Lloyd's two compilation movies of the early Sixties, *Harold*

Harold Lloyd and Eddie Boland

Harold Lloyd and Jobyna Ralston

Lloyd's World of Comedy and *Harold Lloyd's Funny Side of Life*, both of which seemed to hold a great deal of appeal for young people. When, a year before his death in 1971, Lloyd took is 1927 feature *The Kid Brother* out of mothballs and showed it to several university film groups, he was suitably overwhelmed by the enthusiastic response.

The Kid Brother has recently been lauded as Harold Lloyd's masterpiece by more than one film historian. The comedian's next-to-last silent movie, it abounds with wonderful stunts and sight gags that are difficult to describe outside of a detailed plot-synopsis of the movie. And, although nearly all of the gags involve Lloyd with some unusual prop to point up the joke, one (a sailor-suited monkey hilariously clumping around a ship's deck in men's shoes) has the comedian nowhere in sight!

Longer by some twenty minutes than most of Lloyd's Twenties comedy features, *The Kid Brother* perhaps takes longer to build character and audience sympathy, with less footage given over to chase sequences. The setting is a small town named Hickoryville, where Lloyd plays Harold Hickory, a sheriff's misfit youngest son, whose two brothers hulk over him. A droll introductory title informs us that Harold was born on April Fool's Day, adding, "The stork that brought him could hardly fly for laughing."

Harold's a bashful lad whose life seems devoted to serving as a sort of male-Cinderella cook and house-keeper for his more macho siblings and father. When a forbidden medicine show comes to town, Harold, in his father's absence, dons the sheriff's badge and allows them to set up their tents. The show is owned by its dancing distaff attraction, pretty Mary Powers (Jobyna Ralston, a frequent Lloyd leading lady), but it's managed by a pair of scheming tricksters, "Flash" Farrell (Eddie Boland) and Sandoni (Constantine Romanoff), who lusts after Mary. When Harold rescues Mary from the latter's advances, he immediately wins her undying affection. The subsequent storyline is slight, but involves a theft of town funds by the medicine show men, and Harold's eventual recovery of same from a wrecked ship in the bay, where the villains have taken refuge. By the film's close, Harold has not only won the girl, but also gained—for the first time—the respect of his family and friends.

The Kid Brother was filmed under the working-title *The Mountain Boy*, enduring a longer in-production period (eight months) than any of Lloyd's other movies, due to the actor's perfectionism with all aspects of the film. Like Keaton's masterpiece *The General*, *The Kid*

Constantine Romanoff, Harold Lloyd and Jobyna Ralston

Leo Willis, Harold Lloyd and Olin Francis

Brother contains more serious elements than are usually found in Lloyd's work, and offers proof that he was far more than a skilled stunt-actor given to such daredevil accomplishments as hanging from the hands of a precipitously located clock, as in 1923's *Safety Last*. *The Kid Brother* credits the little-remembered Ted Wilde as its director, although it's well known that Lloyd himself, in concert with his gag-writers, had much to do with the *actual* direction of his pictures. But it has been established that *The Kid Brother* had other outside directorial help, including Lewis Milestone (later to achieve fame on his own for such as *All Quiet on the Western Front*).

Harold Lloyd's 1926 feature *For Heaven's Sake* had offered the customary stunt thrills for which the comedian was so popular, and although less well-made a movie than *The Kid Brother*, the former proved more popular with both critics and audiences. Somehow, the actor's fans seemed only to want more gags and chases, with little appreciation for stronger plots and the development of character.

Harold Lloyd and Jobyna Ralston

IT

1927

CREDITS

A Paramount Picture. An Elinor Glyn-Clarence Badger Production. Presented by Adolph Zukor and Jesse L. Lasky. Associate Producer: B. P. Schulberg. Directed by Clarence Badger and (uncredited) Josef von Sternberg. Photographed by H. Kinley Martin. Scenario by Hope Loring and Louis D. Lighton. Titles by George Marion, Jr. Based on a story by Elinor Glyn. Edited by E. Lloyd Sheldon. Seven reels.

CAST

Clara Bow (*Betty Lou Spence*); Antonio Moreno (*Cyrus Waltham*); William Austin (*Monty*); Jacqueline Gadsdon (*Adela Van Norman*); Julia Swayne Gordon (*Mrs. Van Norman*); Priscilla Bonner (*Molly*); Eleanor Lawson (*First Welfare Worker*); Rose Tapley (*Second Welfare Worker*); Elinor Glyn (*Herself*); Gary Cooper (*Newspaper Reporter*).

It didn't make a star of twenty-two-year-old Clara Bow; she had already attained that status in her teens, with a succession of roles in provocatively titled movies like *Daughters of Pleasure* (1924), *The Primrose Path* (1925), *Dancing Mothers* (1926) and—one of her best vehicles—*Mantrap* (1926). But *It*, especially tailored for her talents and personality, was the box-office hit that really solidified Clara's popularity and won her a permanent identification as "The 'IT' Girl."

"It" was nothing more than simple animal magnetism, as publicized by that self-styled high priestess of sex, the British-born sexagenarian grand-dame Elinor Glyn, author of such sizzling filmed novels of 1924 as *Three Weeks* and *His Hour*. Since Madame Glyn had already singled out Paramount contract players Clara Bow and Antonio Moreno as just about the only Hollywood stars of 1926 possessing her idea of "It," Paramount cannily commissioned her to dash off a short novel by that title, paid her $50,000 for the screen rights and quickly turned it into a motion picture teaming Bow and Moreno.

It is a conventional employee-lands-her-boss romantic comedy, with Bow as a vivacious lingerie salesgirl and Moreno the somewhat staid, albeit wealthy and handsome, owner of the department store in which she toils. Nothing is very inventive about *It*'s plot, including the device that serves to delay their getting together: he's led to believe that she's the mother of a "fatherless" child.

William Austin and Gary Cooper.

Clara Bow, Antonio Moreno and unidentified players.

William Austin, Antonio Moreno and Clara Bow

But, as a showcase for Clara Bow's snappy, jazz-age personality and candid sexual warmth, the movie hit the public's fancy at exactly the propitious moment, early in 1927, and the actress's star continued to rise. Four years later, Bow's career would be all but finished, the result of fast living, weight problems and a fragile psyche. But while she remained a hot property, Paramount continued to exploit her appeal in films like *Get Your Man* (1927), *Ladies of the Mob* (1928) and *The Wild Party* (1929).

Clara Bow's importance to the studio was sufficient to allow her to include a brief bit for one of her then-current offscreen loves, Gary Cooper—a fast-rising actor with infinitely more "It" than co-star Antonio Moreno. She was also responsible for freeing Cooper from cowboy roles by getting him cast as her leading man in the subsequent *Children of Divorce* (1927).

Clarence Badger, a Paramount comedy veteran responsible for the direction of most of Will Rogers's silent pictures, as well as Bebe Daniels's *Miss Brewster's Millions* (1926) and the hilarious Raymond Griffith Civil War comedy *Hands Up!* (1926), handled *It* so impressively that Paramount assigned him to direct Clara Bow in two of her four 1928 movies, *Red Hair* and *Three Weekends*. When Badger took ill during production, Josef von Sternberg, one of Paramount's reliable back-ups, was called upon to direct *It*'s final scenes. And this remains among the movies for which Clara Bow is best remembered. Thanks to the combined preservation efforts of Karl Malkames, Patrick Montgomery and Paul Killiam Films, *It* can still be enjoyed and re-evaluated by today's students of film history.

Clara Bow and Antonio Moreno

THE KING OF KINGS

1927

Joseph Striker, Mickey Moore,
H.B. Warner and Ernest Torrence

CREDITS

A Producers Distributing Corp. Picture. Produced and Directed by Cecil B. DeMille. Assistant Directors: Frank Urson, William J. Cowen and Roy Burns. Story and Screenplay by Jeanie Macpherson. Photographed by Peverell Marley, assisted by Fred Westerberg and Jacob A. Badaracco. Color sequences by Technicolor. Edited by Anne Bauchens and Harold McLernon. Associate Editor: Clifford Howard. Art direction by Mitchell Leisen and Anton Grot. Costumes by Earl Luick and Gwen Wakeling. Makeup by Fred C. Ryle. Technical Engineers: Paul Sprunck and Norman Osunn. Researcher: Elizabeth McGaffey. Fourteen reels (copyrighted at eighteen reels).

CAST

H. B. Warner (*Jesus, the Christ*); Dorothy Cumming (*Mary, the Mother*); Ernest Torrence (*Peter*); Joseph Schildkraut (*Judas*); James Neill (*James*); Joseph Striker (*John*); Robert Edeson (*Matthew*); Sidney D'Albrook (*Thomas*); David Imboden (*Andrew*); Charles Belcher (*Philip*); Clayton Packard (*Bartholomew*); Robert Ellsworth (*Simon*); Charles Requa (*James, the Less*); John T. Prince (*Thaddeus*); Jacqueline Logan (*Mary Magdalene*); Rudolph Schildkraut (*Caiaphas, High Priest of Israel*); Sam De Grasse (*The Pharisee*); Casson Ferguson (*The Scribe*); Victor Varconi (*Pontius Pilate, Governor of Judea*); Majel Coleman (*Procula, Wife of Pilate*); Montagu Love (*The Roman Centurion*); William Boyd (*Simon of Cyrene*); Mickey Moore (*Mark*); Theodore Kosloff (*Malchus, Captain of the High Priest's Guard*); George Siegmann (*Barabbas*); Julia Faye (*Martha*); Josephine Norman (*Mary of Bethany*); Kenneth Thomson (*Lazarus*); Alan Brooks (*Satan*); Viola Louie (*The Woman Taken in Adultery*); Muriel McCormac (*The Blind Girl*); Clarence Burton (*Dysmas, the Repentant Thief*); James Mason (*Gestas, the Unrepentant Thief*); May Robson (*The Mother of Gestas*); Dot Farley (*Maid Servant of Caiaphas*); Hector Sarno (*The Galilean Carpenter*); Leon Holmes (*The Imbecile Boy*); Jack Padgen (*Captain of the Roman Guard*); Robert St. Angelo, Redman Finley, James Dime, Richard Alexander, Budd Fine, William De Boar, Robert McKee, Tom London, Edward Schaeffer, Peter Norris and Dick Richards (*Soldiers of Rome*); James Farley (*An Executioner*); Otto Lederer (*Eber, a Pharisee*); Bryant Washburn (*A Young Roman*); Lionel Belmore (*A Roman Noble*); Monte Collins (*A Rich Judean*); Luca Flamma (*A Gallant of Galilee*); Sojin (*A Prince of Persia*); Andre Cheron (*A Wealthy Merchant*); William Costello (*A Babylonian Noble*); Sally Rand (*Slave to Mary Magdalene*); Noble Johnson (*Charioteer*).

In 1923, when producer-director Cecil B. DeMille found the popularity of his lavishly produced dramas and comedies slipping, he turned from the likes of *Male and Female* (1919), *Why Change Your Wife?* (1920) and *Manslaughter* (1922) to a religious theme—and *The Ten Commandments*. Both critics and audiences responded so enthusiastically to that movie that DeMille followed it four years later with a motion picture he had been mentally formulating for many years—a portrayal of Jesus that would obliterate what DeMille termed "the effeminate, sanctimonious, machine-made Christ of Sunday School books." That film, *The King of Kings*, is still considered by many to be the Hollywood showman's finest achievement.

At the time of its release in 1927, *The King of Kings* was also, at the staggering production cost of $2,500,000, second only to the original *Ben-Hur*'s record $4,500,000. DeMille's well-documented obsession with assuring historical accuracies in setting and costume as much as humanly possible (even if historical *plot details* were greatly falsified) would account for much of the expenditure, in addition to its enormous cast and their requisite wardrobe. And the movie ran considerably longer than was then customary. *The King of Kings* was copyrighted at eighteen reels, although the release print ran to a more modest fourteen.

Contemporary critics seem to have come away from this religious spectacle in some sort of born-again trance, inspired to approach their typewriters with unprecedented reverence. But even today, DeMille's *The King of Kings* impresses with the care obviously lavished on every detail of production and most of its acting. However, some of the performances are strictly in the vein of High Camp, with clutching arms, rolling eyeballs and superficially "indicated" emotions. Here the worst offenders are undoubtedly Joseph Schildkraut's treacherous Judas and Jacqueline Logan in her early scenes as Mary Magdalene ("Harness my zebras, gift of the Nubian king!"), prior to her reformation by Jesus. In the latter role, however, H. B. Warner fulfills Cecil B. DeMille's faith in him. As the director once wrote of Warner, "He understood perfectly how I wanted Him portrayed. He had all the virility, tenderness, authority yet restraint, compassion tempered with strength, touch of gentle humor, enjoyment of small and simple things, a divine love of his brethren and enemies alike that the Man of Nazareth must have had." And the public appeared to agree with DeMille's selection. Years later, a minister paid H. B. Warner the supreme compliment: "I saw you in *The King of Kings* as a child, and now, every time I speak of Jesus, it is your face I see."

*Theodore Kosloff, H.B. Warner and unidentified
players*

The film's narrative deals episodically with various
dramatic incidents in the life of Christ, from His redemption of Mary Magdalene, through the raising of Lazarus,
the driving of the moneychangers from the temple, the
Last Supper, the trial before Pilate and the Crucifixion,
concluding with His Resurrection and the Ascension.
Some lengthy sequences were filmed in the primitive
Technicolor hues then prevalent, and they do enhance
the film, even today.

In 1961, Samuel Bronston, a spiritual follower of
DeMille, produced his own *King of Kings*, with the benefit
of widescreen Super Technirama and full-blown Technicolor, and starring the handsome, blue-eyed Jeffrey
Hunter as an unlikely Jesus. Some of it was stirring, but
much of it was solemn and tedious, failing to block out
the memories of those filmgoers who revered the DeMille
version.

H.B. Warner

Richard Arlen

WINGS

1927

CREDITS

A Paramount Picture. Executive Producers: Adolph Zukor and Jesse L. Lasky. Produced by Lucien Hubbard. Associate Producer: B. P. Schulberg. Directed by William A. Wellman. Assistant Director: Norman Z. McLeod. Screenplay by Hope Loring and Louis D. Lighton. Titles by Julian Johnson. Story by John Monk Saunders. Photographed by Harry Perry. Additional photography by E. Burton Steene, Cliff Blackston, Russell Harlan, Bert Baldridge, Frank Cotner, Faxon M. Dean, Ray Olsen, Herman Schoop, L. Guy Wilky and Al Williams. Supervising Editor: E. Lloyd Sheldon. Edited by Lucien Hubbard. Stunt Pilot: Dick Grace. Supervision of the Flying Sequences by S. C. Campbell, Ted Parson, Carl von Hartmann, and James A. Healy. Engineering Effects by Roy Pomeroy. Costumes by Edith Head. Thirteen reels.

CAST

Clara Bow (*Mary Preston*); Charles "Buddy" Rogers (*Jack Powell*); Richard Arlen (*David Armstrong*); Jobyna Ralston (*Sylvia Lewis*); Gary Cooper (*Cadet White*); Arlette Marchal (*Celeste*); El Brendel (*Herman Schwimpf*); Gunboat Smith (*The Sergeant*); Richard Tucker (*Air Commander*); Roscoe Karns (*Lt. Cameron*); Julia Swayne Gordon (*Mrs. Armstrong*); Henry B. Walthall (*Mr. Armstrong*); George Irving (*Mr. Powell*); Hedda Hopper (*Mrs. Powell*); Nigel de Brulier (*Peasant*); James Pierce (*Military Policeman*); Carl von Hartmann (*German Officer*); Dick Grace, Rod Rogers and Tommy Carr (*Aviators*); William Wellman (*Dying Soldier*); Charles Barton (*Doughboy Hit by Ambulance*); Margery Chapin Wellman (*Peasant Woman*); Gloria Wellman (*Peasant Child*).

Charles "Buddy" Rodgers and Clara Bow

William A. ("Wild Bill") Wellman was a World War I veteran and former flying ace with the celebrated Lafayette Flying Corps before working his way up in the motion picture industry from messenger boy to prop man to assistant director. In 1923, he directed his first feature at

Charles "Buddy" Rogers and Richard Arlen

Fox and, three years later, was fortunate enough to be handed the coveted direction of Paramount's large-scale aviation film *Wings*. With Wellman's military background and well-assimilated movie-production knowledge, he so skillfully managed to oversee a large cast, a battery of eleven cameramen, stunt pilots and spectacular battle scenes that *Wings* emerged a worthy successor to MGM's blockbuster 1925 war epic, *The Big Parade*. Indeed, *Wings* proved both a critical favorite and a great crowd-pleaser, and it won a 1927 Best Picture statuette from the Academy of Motion Picture Arts and Sciences during its initial year of existence. The movie also garnered an Academy Award for Roy Pomeroy's "Engineering Effects." In 1929, *Wings* was reissued with sound effects and music.

Clara Bow and unidentified players

Richard Tucker, Charles "Buddy"
Rogers and Richard Arlen

Richard Arlen and Gary Cooper

Richard Arlen and Charles "Buddy" Rogers

Wings made immediate stars of its two male leads, Charles "Buddy" Rogers and Richard Arlen. Top-billed Clara Bow, of course, was already a big box-office draw, which explains her headline positioning in the film's credits, despite the limited amount of footage in which she appears. And Gary Cooper's one-scene cameo reflects the speed with which, in 1927, he became a leading man.

Much of the movie was shot in San Antonio, Texas, home of America's first military airfield, where Wellman incurred the displeasure of Paramount executives by insisting on waiting for the right combinations of sun and clouds for the thrilling aerial-combat scenes that so dominate the film and have seldom since been equalled. For its New York opening, *Wings* featured Paramount's wide-screen Magnascope process, which spread its projection across the entire stage-opening. The addition of color tinting in some of the airborne battle scenes highlighted the blue skies and spouts of orange flame shooting from the downed planes.

Wings holds up less successfully, nearly sixty years later, in its dramatic scenes, especially those concerned with the romantic entanglements involving Bow's unrequited (until the film's end) affection for Rogers. He, in turn, goes for Jobyna Ralston, who really loves Arlen! But the movie's *real* love story is the bond of friendship that grows, after a hostile start, between Arlen and Rogers. This culminates in a climax of contrived irony when Arlen is shot down behind German lines. He manages to escape in an enemy plane—only to be shot down by Rogers, who thinks he's *avenging* Arlen. The latter's death scene, cradled in the arms of a devastated Rogers, who kisses him on the mouth, reflects the unabashed sentimentality of an era far removed from our own.

Today, *Wings* remains among the few great motion pictures about World War I, and recently it became the first major-studio *silent* film to be issued on videocassette. For the record, its director, William Wellman, is also the man responsible for a pair of the *Second* World War's finest movies, *The Story of G. I. Joe* (1945) and *Battleground* (1949).

THE CAT AND THE CANARY

1927

Martha Mattox and Laura La Plante

CREDITS

A Universal Picture. Presented by Carl Laemmle. Directed by Paul Leni. Screenplay by Alfred A. Cohn and Robert F. Hill. Titles by Walter Anthony. Based on the stage play by John Willard. Photographed by Gilbert Warrenton. Art Direction by Charles D. Hall. Eight reels.

CAST

Laura La Plante (*Annabelle West*); Creighton Hale (*Paul Jones*); Forrest Stanley (*Charles Wilder*); Tully Marshall (*Roger Crosby*); Gertrude Astor (*Cecily Young*); Flora Finch (*Susan Sillsby*); Arthur Edmund Carewe (*Harry Blythe*); Martha Mattox (*"Mammy" Pleasant*); Lucien Littlefield (*The Doctor*); George Siegmann (*Hendricks*); Joe Murphy (*Milkman*); Billy Engle (*Taxi Driver*).

Lucien Littlefield and Laura La Plante

This first screen adaptation of John Willard's popular mystery comedy, a Broadway hit of 1922, became the prototype for any number of subsequent haunted-house thrillers featuring a frightened heroine threatened by a heavily disguised (or unseen) killer. Its plot is simple: family members of the late eccentric Cyrus Vance gather in a forbidding old mansion for the reading of his will at midnight, just twenty years after his death. But the joke is on them, for Vance knew they all thought him crazy, and so disinherited the lot—all except for his most distant surviving relative, young Annabelle West (Laura La Plante), who will become his heiress if she survives the night in West's house, with her sanity intact. As the attendant would-have-been heirs settle in for the night, there ensues the expected elements of ghostly unrest, with mysterious clawlike hands clutching at the guests from behind secret panels and an eerie atmosphere of impending doom, augmented by the sinister characterizations of housekeeper Martha Mattox and bogus doctor Lucien Littlefield.

Paul Leni, who had been directing films in his native Germany since 1916—and was then best known internationally for the 1924 horror-fantasy *Das Wachsfigurenkabinett* (*Waxworks*)—was imported in 1927 by Universal's Carl Laemmle to add his stylish expertise to *The Cat and the Canary*. It was a wise move, for Leni's earlier background in set design, coupled with a penchant for unusual lighting, offbeat camera angles and the clever superimposition of visual images, caused this chiller to stand out from all of its contemporary competition, and

Laura La Plante

Flora Finch, Gertrude Astor, Creighton Hale, Forrest Stanley, Laura La Plante and Arthur Edmund Carewe

laid the groundwork for no less than three remakes and a brilliant spoof of the genre, James Whale's 1932 classic, *The Old Dark House*. But the 1927 *The Cat and the Canary* works least well in its scenes of comic relief, and although its eerie atmosphere has weathered the years well, its humor has not, especially with regard to its bumbling hero, portrayed by the tiresome Creighton Hale, who is hardly a match for his 1939 counterpart, Bob Hope. Twelve years after the silent Leni classic, haunted-mansion thrills had become so clichéd that Hope's engaging wit was needed to make a talkie hit of the hoary old John Willard melodrama. Its first remake, Rupert Julian's negligible early-sound version, was retitled *The Cat Creeps*, and is only slightly less well remembered than Radley Metzger's somewhat kinky,

British-made 1978 adaptation, which reverted to the play's original title.

Leni's 1927 cast served their quirky characters with all the red-herring requirements of the Alfred A. Cohn-Robert F. Hill screenplay, with Laura La Plante appropriately lovely and fearful in the story's pivotal role of the heiress who wears her gem-heavy necklace to bed. Somehow, she seems to deserve better than goofy Creighton Hale. But Paul Leni's dexterity with uncanny plots like this one is what makes the movie work so beautifully, and a retrospective look at this *The Cat and the Canary* rewards the astute viewer with its appropriately bizarre use of imaginative camerawork, lighting and stagecraft. The result is macabre story-telling of remarkable visual ingenuity.

SUNRISE

1927

Janet Gaynor and George O'Brien

George O'Brien

CREDITS

A Fox Film. Presented by William Fox. Directed by F. W. Murnau. Assistant Director: Herman Bing. Scenario by Carl Mayer. Titles by Katherine Hilliker and H. H. Caldwell. Based on the story *Die Reise nach Tilsit* ("A Trip to Tilsit") by Hermann Sudermann. Photographed by Charles Rosher and Karl Struss. Assistant Photographers: Hal Carney and Stuart Thompson. Production designed by Rochus Gliese. Assistant Art Directors: Edgar G. Ulmer and Alfred Metscher. Edited by Katherine Hilliker and H. H. Caldwell. Synchronized Musical Score by Hugo Riesenfeld. Sound effects by Movietone. Nine reels.

CAST

George O'Brien (*The Man*); Janet Gaynor (*The Wife*); Margaret Livingston (*The Woman from the City*); Bodil Rosing (*The Maid*); J. Farrell MacDonald (*The Photographer*); Ralph Sipperly (*The Barber*); Jane Winton (*The Manicure Girl*); Arthur Housman (*The Obtrusive Gentleman*); Eddie Boland (*The Obliging Gentleman*); Gibson Gowland (*The Angry Motorist*); F. W. Murnau (*Vacationer on Boat*); Sally Eilers, Gino Corrado, Barry Norton and Robert Kortman (*Bit Players*).

Margaret Livingston

Janet Gaynor

Sunrise, subtitled "A Song of Two Humans," was undoubtedly one of 1927's most artistic and beautiful motion pictures, and its reputation as a true classic is well deserved. At the first Academy Awards, covering 1927–28, *Sunrise* took three statuettes: one for "Artistic Quality of Production" (a curious category quite separate from Best Picture, and one that was discontinued the next year); second, for the striking cinematography of Charles Rosher and Karl Struss; and a third, for Best Actress Janet Gaynor. Reflecting the changes that have occurred since those first awards, Gaynor's citation was not only for *Sunrise*, but also for two other performances—in *Seventh Heaven* (1927) and *Street Angel* (1928).

The film's German-born director, F. W. Murnau, was one of many European artists whose work abroad had impressed and influenced Hollywood craftsmen and studio bosses. Murnau had begun directing in 1919 in Germany, focusing on material of the macabre and bizarre. But while his colleagues embraced the current vogue for expressionistic sets, decor and lighting, Murnau chose to employ realistic backgrounds to offset his world of the fantastic. Notable examples of his early artistry apear in 1920's *Der Januskopf* (based on *Dr. Jekyll and Mr. Hyde*), *Schloss Vogelöd* (*Haunted Castle*) and, most enduring of all, the vampire classic *Nosferatu*. William Fox, who signed Murnau to an American contract, was even more impressed with 1924's *Der letzte Mann* (*The Last Laugh*) and *Faust* (1926), and he offered the director freedom to choose his own subject, a generous budget and the opportunity to work without interference. It has also been reported that Fox never even saw *Sunrise* until its completion.

The plot of *Sunrise* is deceptively simple, with all details of its time and place kept indistinct, although we sense that we're in some foreign locale. But, in true allegorical fashion, the settings are an unnamed country village and an equally anonymous city. Not even the leading characters have specific names. The husband (George O'Brien), a ruggedly attractive young farmer, meets a sophisticated city woman (Margaret Livingston) who's vacationing in the country, and they enter into an affair, during which she tries to persuade him to kill his wife, leave his home and relocate to the city with her. Temporarily obsessed with this vamp, he is sufficiently influenced to carry out that plan, and invites his wife (Janet Gaynor) on a picnic outing in their rowboat. Planning to make her murder seem an "accident," he takes her out but is unable to execute his scheme, and only succeeds in frightening her with his irrational behavior. Terrified, the wife runs away from his efforts to reassure her of his love, and boards a

Janet Gaynor and George O'Brien

Arthur Housman, Janet Gaynor and George O'Brien

Janet Gaynor and George O'Brien

streetcar into the city, where he follows her. That evening, having reconciled, they enjoy the amusements of Luna Park. En route home, a dangerous storm arises and their boat capsizes. The husband reaches the embankment, but his wife now appears to have drowned, after all. Distraught with grief, he's again approached by the city woman, who thinks he has carried out their plan, and on whom he turns all of his anger and frustration, brutalizing her and threatening to kill her. But then a happy outcry signals that the wife has been found alive, and the couple is joyously reunited, while the temptress is left to return to her city alone.

Murnau filmed all of this with great creativity, inspiring George O'Brien to give probably the finest, most sensitive performance of his career (the latter part of which would be devoted to Westerns and outdoor action dramas). Blond-wigged Janet Gaynor's expressive pantomime here helped her win her Academy Award.

But much of one's vivid memory of this haunting film is wrapped up in its *visual* individuality, and for that the credit is equally due master-cinematographers Charles Rosher and Karl Struss, shooting on the costly studio sets of Murnau's hand-picked designer, Rochus Gliese. With the collaboration of these brilliant craftsmen, Murnau magically combined elements of both naturalism and distorted expressionistic images augmented by an uncanny deployment of lighting and double exposure. By so doing, he made their surroundings illuminate the psychological feelings of his few central characters. And his subtle use of symbolism was brilliantly devised.

Karl Struss later recalled his copacetic association with Charles Rosher on this film with the comment, "Murnau left the whole visual side of the picture to us; he concentrated entirely on the actors." Janet Gaynor, in turn, has spoken of the electric tension that prevailed on that set. "I adored him," she remarked of her director, who apparently favored her, for she conceded, "I was told by people who could understand German that he was very, very cruel to them in his language, but he was marvelous to me."

Like many of the screen's great classics, *Sunrise* was admired by many of its contemporary critics, but failed to draw enough filmgoers to achieve box-office success.

George O'Brien and Janet Gaynor.

George O'Brien
and Margaret Livingston

Dolores Del Rio

LOVES OF CARMEN

1927

CREDITS

A Fox Film. Presented by William Fox. Directed by Raoul Walsh. Assistant Director: Archibald Buchanan. Scenario by Gertrude Orr. Titles by Katherine Hilliker and H. H. Caldwell. Based on the novel by Prosper Mérimée. Photographed by Lucien Andriot and John Marta. Edited by Katherine Hilliker and H. H. Caldwell. Nine reels.

CAST

Dolores Del Rio (*Carmen*); Don Alvarado (*José*); Victor McLaglen (*Escamillo*); Nancy Nash (*Michaela*); Rafael Valverda (*Miguel*); Mathilde Comont (*Emilia*); Jack Baston (*Morales*); Carmen Costello (*Teresa*); Fred Kohler (*Gypsy Chief*).

Prosper Mérimée's gypsy *femme fatale* Carmen probably outranks both Cleopatra and Camille as the mantrap most frequently portrayed in movies over the years. During the Teens, the role was interpreted on the American screen alone by Marguerite Snow, Marion Leonard, Geraldine Farrar, Edna Purviance (in Chaplin's burlesque version), Theda Bara and Pola Negri. But most authentic of all was undoubtedly the remarkably beautiful Mexican star Dolores Del Rio, who portrayed Carman in Fox's 1927 remake of their 1915 Theda Bara film.

That fascinating Spanish gypsy survives most durably, of course, in the Georges Bizet opera *Carmen*, which remains among the most popular works in the French repertoire. But even without Bizet's melodious music, that temptress is so vivid and compelling that actresses and audiences alike have been consistently attracted by her wiles over the years. And if Dolores Del Rio's elegant physiognomy and refined beauty innately bring too much breeding to the role, then the actress herself—obviously inspired by both the story and her director, Raoul Walsh—insinuates herself into the part with such verisimilitude that the viewer is hard-pressed to imagine anyone else portraying Carmen.

Mérimée's familiar story undergoes little variation in this vigorous adaptation. Carmen is still an employee in a Spanish cigar factory at the outset. Attracting the ardor of both Escamillo (Victor McLaglen), the flamboyant bullfighter, and José (Don Alvarado), a young officer, she pits the latter against his Commander, who lusts after her himself. Carmen precipitates a duel between the two men, and the superior officer is killed. Carmen and José

Don Alvarado and Dolores Del Rio

Mathilde Comont, Dolores Del Rio and unidentified players

flee to the mountains, where they hide out together. But the wanton one soon tires of this relationship, and she restlessly wanders off to the city bullfights, where she quickly becomes Escamillo's mistress. Learning of this development José follows her to the bullring, where he stabs her to death.

Fox evidently lavished a generous budget on this *Loves of Carmen*, for its excellent sets and costumes reflect taste and care. Gertrude Orr's scenario mines more humor from the torrid plot than one generally gets in other *Carmens*, and this undoubtedly reflects the personality of its director Raoul Walsh. Walsh had scored a major success with the previous year's *What Price Glory?*, two of whose stars (Del Rio and McLaglen) he again directed here, which might account for the excellence of their self-confident performances. Indeed, Dolores Del Rio's wonderfully uninhibited acting (not customarily the hallmark of her screen work) tells us about the unquestioning trust that she must have placed in Walsh. The result is a Carmen without equal, certainly not surpassed by the tantalizing but somewhat less fiery temptress of another Latin beauty, Rita Hayworth, in a 1948 Technicolor remake, *The Loves of Carmen*.

Victor McLaglen and Dolores Del Rio

THE LAST COMMAND

1928

William Powell and Emil Jannings

Unidentified player and Emil Jannings

CREDITS

A Paramount Picture. Presented by Adolph Zukor and Jesse L. Lasky. Production supervised by Joseph G. Bachmann. Associate Producer: B. P. Schulberg. Directed by Josef von Sternberg. Screenplay by John F. Goodrich, from an original story by Sternberg. Based on an incident related to Lajos Biro by Ernst Lubitsch. Titles by Herman J. Mankiewicz. Photographed by Bert Glennon. Edited by William Shea. Set Design by Hans Dreier. Technical Director: Nicholas Kobyliansky. Nine reels.

CAST

Emil Jannings (*General Dolgorucki/Grand Duke Sergius Alexander*); Evelyn Brent (*Natacha Dobrowa*); William Powell (*Leo Andreiev*); Nicholas Soussanin (*The Adjutant*); Michael Visaroff (*Serge, the Valet*); Jack Raymond (*Assistant Director*); Viacheslav Savitsky (*A Private*); Fritz Feld (*A Revolutionist*); Harry Semels (*Soldier Extra*); Alexander Ikonnikov and Nicholas Kobyliansky (*Drillmasters*).

Josef von Sternberg is best remembered as the man who virtually created Marlene Dietrich, as we know her today, in all those exotic, beautifully photographed sex dramas of the Thirties, from the German-made *The Blue Angel* (1930) to *The Devil Is a Woman* (1935). Before that, in the Twenties at Paramount, he was busy creating a small but unique handful of motion pictures characterized by careful attention to the filmic images of light and shadow, often filtered with smoke and mist, usually encasing a story of a dark-hued content. Obsessed with the underworld milieu, Sternberg created a gangster-world of his own imagination that bore little resemblance to reality in such films as *Underworld* (1927), *The Docks of New York* (1928) and *Thunderbolt* (1929). Amidst these movies, however, he also turned out *The Last Command*, the compelling and fact-based story of a former Czarist general reduced to working as an extra in the Hollywood studios. This role was rightly considered perfect for Emil Jannings, the distinguished character actor Paramount had borrowed from Germany's Ufa organization, following his great successes in *The Last Laugh* (1924), *Variety* (1925) and *Faust* (1926). Jannings stayed in the U.S. long enough to star in a total of six films, the best of which were *The Last Command* and *The Way of All Flesh* (1927), for the combination of which he won the motion picture Academy's first Best Actor award for the 1927–28 season.

Emil Jannings

Evelyn Brent, William Powell, Nicholas Soussanin and Emil Jannings.

The Last Command was originally shot under the working-title of *The General*, which was, unfortunately, the better-known name of one of Buster Keaton's best recent vehicles. And, as a title, of course *The Last Command* has a far more dramatic ring to it.

In this film, Jannings portrays the elderly Sergius Alexander, formerly the Imperialist Russian General Dolgorucki, before he was overthrown by the Revolutionists, who has drifted to the American movie capital. When he can get the work, he now makes $7.50 a day as an extra. As such, his big moment comes when the Russian-born film director Leo Andreiev (William Powell), recognizing him from a photograph, realizes that this is the man who once took a whip to him in 1914 Russia, where Andreiev was an impoverished actor-revolutionist. And so, for the screen, Sergius Alexander is engaged, at a pittance, to be a general again and lead an army of movie-Russians. Confusing reality and make-believe, the old man reenacts a segment from his own past, "becoming" again the Russian general confronted with his own troops in revolt. Repeating the past against a fake Hollywood-studio background, the ex-general increasingly believes that the scene is real, and he actually *lives* the character, thinking that the old Russia of the Czars had returned. But it is all too much for the old man, and he falls dead in the "snow," his epitaph ironically delivered by a nearby studio casting director: "He was a great actor, that old guy."

Evelyn Brent

Evelyn Brent

The Last Command offered Jannings a wonderful role and, under Sternberg's guidance, he delivered a magnificent performance, followed closely by the work of William Powell, in a double-edged part, and the fascinatingly intense Evelyn Brent (the unforgettable "Feathers" of Sternberg's *Underworld*), whose scenes occur in extensive flashbacks as the old man recalls Natacha, the Bolshevik spy with whom he had once conducted a complex emotional relationship, before witnessing her death in a train accident.

Some of those in Paramount's hierarchy had misgivings about the bitterly ironic commentary on Hollywood filmmaking with which Sternberg had filled *The Last Command*, and they tried to block its release—until cooler heads prevailed. In addition to Jannings's award, the Academy of Motion Picture Arts and Sciences also accorded this movie a Best Picture nomination. But the winner, understandably, was the far more popular *Wings*.

THE CROWD

1928

James Murray and Eleanor Boardman

James Murray

CREDITS

A Metro-Goldwyn-Mayer Picture. Directed by King Vidor. Scenario by King Vidor, John V. A. Weaver and Harry Behn. Titles by Joe Farnham. Photographed by Henry Sharp. Edited by Hugh Wynn. Art Direction by Cedric Gibbons and Arnold Gillespie. Nine reels.

CAST

Eleanor Boardman (*Mary Sims*); James Murray (*John Sims*); Bert Roach (*Bert*); Estelle Clark (*Jane*); Daniel G. Tomlinson (*Jim*); Dell Henderson (*Dick*); Lucy Beaumont (*Mother*); Freddie Burke Frederick (*Junior*); Alice Mildred Puter (*Daughter*); Sally Eilers (*Girl at Party*).

In his 1953 autobiography *A Tree Is a Tree*, director King Vidor recalls how *The Crowd* grew out of a casual conversation that transpired between him and MGM executive Irving Thalberg, who inquired what Vidor might do as a follow-up to his then-current hit *The Big Parade*. Vidor suggested a drama about the average man, and was encouraged to develop a scenario—which he soon did, with the assistance of writers John V. A. Weaver and Harry Behn.

John Sims (James Murray), a born dreamer, becomes one of an enormous battery of New York City office workers, human machines that spend their nine-to-five days adding up figures and watching the clock. But John alleviates his boring job by secretly drafting advertising slogans, one of which he hopes will someday make a success of him. On a blind double-date with his friend Bert (Bert Roach) and Bert's girl Jane (Estelle Clark), John meets Mary (Eleanor Boardman) and, as they ride down Fifth Avenue on a double-decker bus, he points out a "clown" juggling balls to publicize a restaurant. "I'll bet his mother thought he was going to be President of the United States," cracks John, heralding a later scene in which he, too, will be reduced to similar circumstances.

The couples go to Coney Island and, on the way home, John proposes and Mary accepts. They honeymoon at Niagara Falls, returning to settle down in a modest Manhattan flat that looks out on the noisy elevated transit system. A visit from Mary's disapproving mother and two brothers sends John out into the night for gin, but when he returns it's hours later and he's drunk.

Five years later, Bert has been promoted, but John's still a clerk with only an $8.00 raise during that time. He

Eleanor Boardman and James Murray

and Mary now have two children, a girl and boy. Then John wins five hundred dollars in a slogan-writing contest, but his elation is cut short when their little daughter is run down by a truck and dies. Unable to shake off this tragedy, John loses his job and becomes a door-to-door salesman. At home, he quarrels with Mary. She heeds her family's advice to leave John, who contemplates suicide, but a comment from his accompanying son stops him in time. Returning home, he finds that Mary was unable to stay away, after all. John takes his little family to a vaudeville show, where the movie's final sequence views them laughing in enjoyment, along with the rest of the audience.

The Crowd has been justly acclaimed, over the years, as one of the enduring classics of the American silent screen. The film's strength lies in its naturalistic simplicity, its beauty in the truth Vidor draws from the average and the commonplace. John is everyman, and Mary is everywoman. Their clothing looks as real as their surroundings—the New York City streets and tenements where Vidor took his cast and crew to maintain a sense of ordinary actuality. But he also made some use of distorted sets and contrived perspectives to achieve other effects, all of which add up to a motion picture of power and feeling that only wavers momentarily with overemphatic touches of sentiment, flashes of melodramatic acting and a few minor clichés that are easy to overlook.

Vidor's choice of his stars was cunning, for he realized that casting a recognizable Hollywood actor as John would detract from the semidocumentary atmosphere he had in mind. And so he drew a reluctant James Murray from the extra ranks and made him a star. Murray had been a movie-theatre doorman, a dishwasher and a railrider, and confessed to Vidor that he didn't even know if he could act. But Vidor proved that by drawing an extraordinarily believable performance from him. In the year The Crowd sat on MGM's shelf awaiting release, Murray played other leading roles for the studio. But success proved difficult for him, and he gained the deserved reputation of a chronic and unreliable alcoholic. The roles got smaller, and the films less important. At thirty-five, he was found dead in New York's Hudson River, the cause unknown.

If James Murray deserves to be remembered for his fine work in The Crowd, then so does Eleanor Boardman, a serenely lovely actress whose Mary cannot help but hold an audience's sympathy as she attempts to

Eleanor Boardman and James Murray

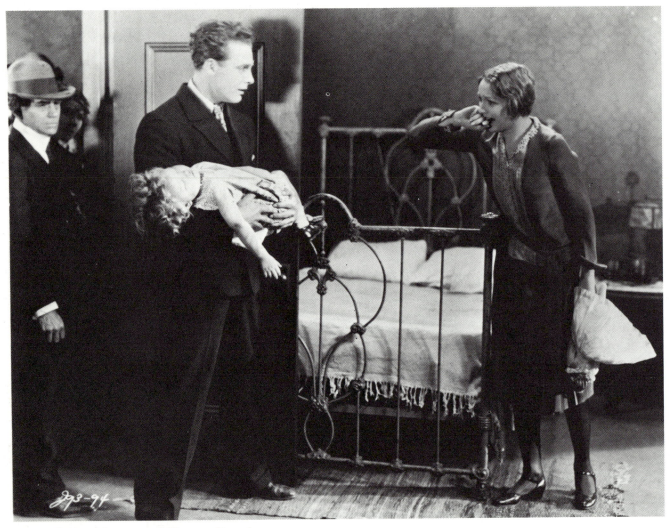

James Murray and Eleanor Boardman

cope with the loss of a child, and a husband who will never really amount to anything. But *The Crowd* is never as bleak as the preceding synopsis may sound; John and Mary have their lighter moments, too, some of which are enhanced by Bert Roach's good-natured performance as John's friend.

King Vidor carefully paints this moving picture in many shades of gray, frequently sidestepping the obvious pitfalls of figurative blacks and whites that would have made *The Crowd* all too grim and unrelenting for 1928's blindly optimistic audiences. Vidor fought MGM to keep the film from concluding on too optimistic a note (several different endings are said to have been shot), and the one described above would seem to offer hope, but no solutions.

Oddly enough, in that first year of the Academy Awards, *The Crowd* drew no nominations for either of its leading actors' striking performances, although it did win Vidor a nod for his direction (Frank Borzage was the winner for a vastly more popular film called *Seventh Heaven*), and the film was mentioned for "artistic quality of production." *The Crowd* wasn't a box-office winner in 1928, although it did manage to break even. But today its classic status is undisputed.

TEMPEST

1928

Camilla Horn and John Barrymore

John Barrymore

CREDITS

A United Artists Picture. A Joseph M. Schenck Production. Produced by John W. Considine, Jr. Directed by Sam Taylor and (uncredited) Viachetslav Tourjansky and Lewis Milestone. Screenplay by C. Gardner Sullivan and (uncredited) Erich von Stroheim and Lewis Milestone. Based on a story by V. I. Nemirovich-Dantchenko. Photographed by Charles Rosher. Art Direction by William Cameron Menzies. Costumes by Alice O'Neill. Musical Score by Hugo Riesenfeld. Ten reels.

CAST

John Barrymore (*Sergeant Ivan Markov*); Camilla Horn (*Princess Tamara*); Louis Wolheim (*Sergeant Bulba*); Boris De Fas (*The Peddler*); George Fawcett (*The General*); Ullrich Haupt (*The Captain*); Michael Visaroff (*The Guard*); Lena Malena (*Tamara's Friend*).

As the silent-film era waned in the late Twenties, matinee idol John Barrymore topped a box-office poll of American movie theatres, reflecting the public's enthusiastic response to his romantic flamboyance in such dramatic ventures as *Don Juan* (1926), *The Sea Beast* (1926) and *When a Man Loves* (1927). Under a three-picture contract with United Artists, Barrymore ended his non-talking career with a brace of costume dramas opposite the ash-blond German beauty, Camilla Horn: *Tempest* (1928) and *Eternal Love* (1929).

In *Tempest*, a stirring tale of peasant-aristocrat love against a background of that once-popular Hollywood subject, the Russian Revolution, Barrymore offers a superbly controlled performance—especially since first-hand reports indicate that he was drunk throughout much of the filming. But even in a lengthy prison sequence, the actor remains in full command of his considerable talent, limning the mental deterioration brought on by prolonged incarceration with extraordinary skill. Undoubtedly, Ivan Markov, the peasant soldier who ruined his army career for love of a general's daughter, ranks among Barrymore's finest silent-screen performances. And he's well matched by the expressive Camilla Horn, as well as character actors George Fawcett (as her father, the general), Louis Wolheim (Ivan's sergeant-friend and the film's leavening device), Ullrich Haupt (the heroine's rigid suitor), and—most charismatic of them all—Boris De Fas (the sinister peddler and future revolutionary). This in-

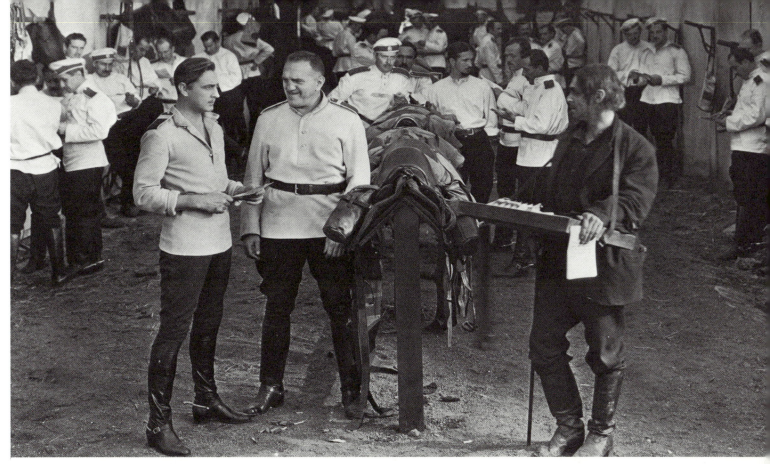

John Barrymore, Louis Wolheim and Boris De Fas

tense, gap-toothed actor's ugly-handsome visage brings to mind an odd blending of Paul Muni and Charles Manson.

As a film, *Tempest* is fairly routine romantic melodrama. But Charles Rosher's strikingly beautiful black-and-white photography reflects his skill at lighting the excellent sets of designer William Cameron Menzies, as well as his actors. At forty-five, Barrymore is made to seem at least fifteen years younger, courtesy of Rosher's soft-focus artistry.

Fortunately, *Tempest*'s checkered production history isn't reflected on the screen. Originally, it was intended as an Erich von Stroheim vehicle, then rewritten for Barrymore. For his leading lady, production chief Joseph M. Schenck first tried to cast Barrymore's current love, Dolores Costello, but was unable to obtain her services from Warner Bros. And so starlet Carole Lombard won the role, but had to bow out when an automobile accident required facial plastic surgery. *Tempest* began filming, under the direction of Russia's Viachetslav Tourjansky, with the brunette Dorothy Sebastian as Tamara. But when it was decided that Tourjansky's approach was too arty and his pace too deliberate, both he and his leading lady left the project. Briefly, Lewis Milestone took over the direction, but Sam Taylor soon succeeded Milestone, and his is the name eventually credited with *Tempest*'s direction. To replace Dorothy Sebastian, Schenck cast from his own couch. Fortunately, his mistress Camilla Horn could act, and played well against Barrymore.

Like most pre-talkies, *Tempest* is little-remembered today, but its current availability on videocassette should assure its rediscovery.

Camilla Horn, George Fawcett and John Barrymore

LIGHTS OF NEW YORK

1928

*Helene Costello, Wheeler Oak-
man and Gladys Brockwell*

Robert Elliott, Gladys Brockwell, Cullen Landis and Helene Costello

CREDITS

A Warner Bros.-Vitaphone Picture. Directed by Bryan Foy. Screenplay by Hugh Herbert and Murray Roth. Photographed by E. H. Dupar. Edited by Jack Killifer. Sound by Vitaphone. Seven reels.

CAST

Helene Costello (*Kitty Lewis*); Cullen Landis (*Eddie Morgan*); Gladys Brockwell (*Molly Thompson*); Mary Carr (*Mrs. Morgan*); Wheeler Oakman (*Hawk Miller*); Eugene Pallette (*Gene*); Robert Elliott (*Detective Crosby*); Tom Dugan (*Sam*); Tom McGuire (*Collins*); Guy D'Ennery (*Tommy*); Walter Percival (*Mr. Jackson*); Jere Delaney (*Mr. Dickson*).

Pure novelty is what sold Warner Bros.' *Lights of New York* to an intrigued public in mid-1928. It has been said to have cost a modest $75,000 and, without any star names to "sell" it, brought in a then-sensational million-plus at the box-office. Its gimmick: this otherwise routine gangster yarn—and not Al Jolson's legendary *The Jazz Singer*—was the first *all-talking* feature-length motion picture. As such, it was, in *every* sense of the word, a pioneering effort. The film's use of gangsters and a backstage nightclub setting indicated that screenwriters Hugh Herbert and Murray Roth had been influenced by the long-running, current stage hit *Broadway* (which itself would reach the screen in 1929).

Incredibly, *Lights of New York* had started out to be nothing more than a two-reel Vitaphone short, but had gradually snow-balled in length until it was suddenly a fifty-seven-minute feature talkie. Where 1927's *The Jazz Singer* had boasted only song numbers and talking sequences, this movie talked from start to finish, albeit in a fashion bearing little resemblance to natural everyday speech! Because of the static placement of concealed and immobile microphones, actors who moved while delivering dialogue had to prolong their words with great deliberation until they reached the next mike, with line readings like "Take him...for...a ride."

Its storyline—about two small-town barbers (Cullen Landis and Eugene Pallette) who move to Manhattan, where bootleggers soon make their shop a cover for illegal operations—offered nothing new. One barber becomes the boyfriend of a nightclub dancer (Helene Costello), and when her boss (Wheeler Oakman), the

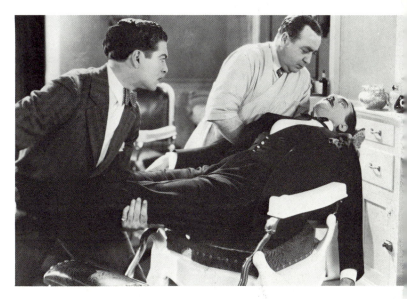

Cullen Landis, Eugene Pallette and Wheeler Oakman

chief bootlegger, is murdered with her gun, she's accused of the crime. Later, the real killer turns out to be the deceased's cast-off mistress (Gladys Brockwell), and the lovers leave New York's corruption for a more bucolic (and presumably safer) future elsewhere.

Granting its attendant problems as a landmark talking picture, *Lights of New York* is nevertheless a perfectly awful movie. Apart from the accomplished Gladys Brockwell (and, to a lesser degree, detective Robert Elliott) the acting is rather hopeless—which might explain why few readers of this book will be familiar with the short-lived careers of Helene Costello and Cullen Landis. And to accommodate the problem-beset sound-recording engineers, director Bryan Foy obviously obeyed the edict that a monotone delivery recorded best. None of which helped the story rife with the melodramatic activity of chorines, gangsters and bootleggers—hardly a background for slow-paced action.

But crude as it is, *Lights of New York* brought a revolution to the industry. For the silent screen, 1928 was suddenly twilight time.

LILAC TIME

1928

Gary Cooper and Colleen Moore

Colleen Moore and Gary Cooper

CREDITS

A First National Picture. Produced by John McCormick. Directed by George Fitzmaurice. Scenario by Carey Wilson and Willis Goldbeck. Titles by George Marion, Jr. Based on the play by Jane Cowl and Jane Murfin. Photographed by Sidney Hickok. Aerial Photography by Alvin Knechtel. Art Direction by Horace Jackson. Edited by Al Hall. Music by Nathaniel Shilkret. Song: "Jeannine, I Dream of Lilac Time" by L. Wolfe Gilbert. Technical Advisors: Cullen Tate, Dick Grace, Capt. L. J. S. Scott, Capt. Robert de Couedic and Harry Redmond. Musical score and sound effects by Vitaphone. Eleven reels.

CAST

Colleen Moore (*Jeannine Berthelot*); Gary Cooper (*Captain Philip Blythe*); Burr McIntosh (*General Blythe*); George Cooper (*Mechanic's Helper*); Cleve Moore (*Captain Russell*); Kathryn McGuire (*Lady Iris Rankin*); Eugenie Besserer (*Madame Berthelot*); Emile Chautard (*Burgomaster of Berle Les Boise*); Jack Stone (*The Kid*); Edward Dillon (*Mike, the Mechanic*); Arthur Lake (*The Unlucky One*); Dick Grace, Stuart Knox, Harlan Hilton, Richard Jarvis, Jack Ponder and Dan Dowling (*Aviators*); Edward Clayton (*The Enemy Ace*); Paul Hurst (*Hospital Orderly*); Philo McCullough (*German Officer*); Nelson McDowell (*A French Drummer*).

Gary Cooper and Colleen Moore

With the resurgence of World War I themes in movies of the mid-to-late Twenties (*The Big Parade, What Price Glory?, Wings*) inevitably came the Great Love Story, a perfect example of which was *Lilac Time*. Produced on an impressive scale by John McCormick, it was a perfect vehicle for his talented wife, Colleen Moore. The actress was best known for her comedy roles, although her serious dramatic work in 1924's *So Big* had confirmed a latent ability to portray strong emotions and wring empathetic reactions from her audience.

But *Lilac Time*, in which Moore is scarcely ever offscreen (except for some aerial dogfight footage) allows her a wide range of expression, from pratfall humor to expressing the devastating loss of a loved one. In his third year of filmmaking, Gary Cooper—on his first loan-out from Paramount—fits well into the role of her romantic teammate. Perhaps it was the smooth, seasoned direction

of George Fitzmaurice that helped the actor overcome an awkward stiffness that had infused much of his earlier acting.

Adapted from the 1917 Jane Cowl-Jane Murfin stage play (they also collaborated on *Smilin' Through*), *Lilac Time* is set in and around a French village near the front, amid the Great War. Jeannine (Moore), known as "Jeannie" to the seven British aviators billeted at her family's sprawling farmhouse, has become their unofficial mascot. When one of the group dies in a plane crash, he's replaced by Capt. Philip Blythe (Cooper), whom Jeannie first encounters on a mutually antagonistic level. It's some time before they come to appreciate each other's more attractive qualities, but from then on it's romance of the chaste variety that frequently prevailed in the Twenties, long before audiences learned to expect bare torsos and rumpled bedsheets.

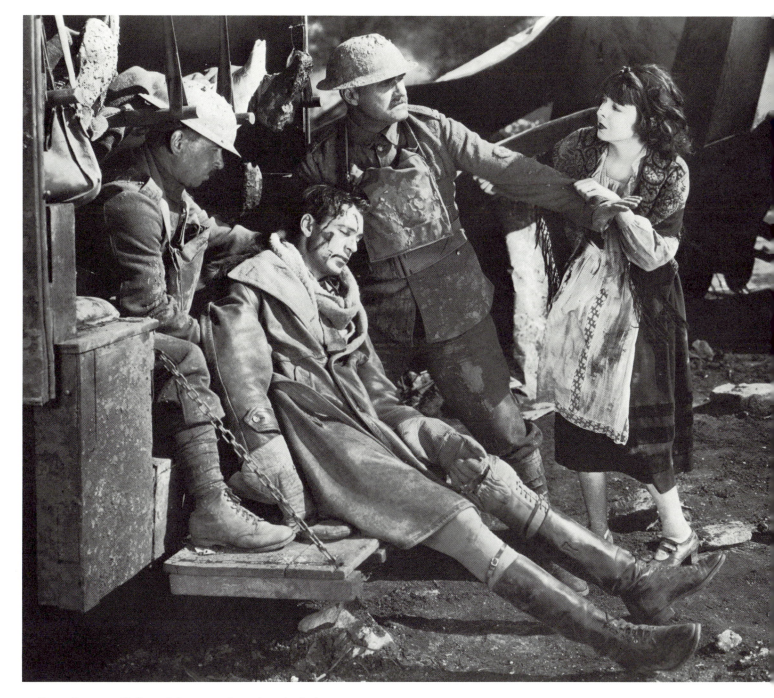

Gary Cooper, Colleen Moore and unidentified players

Inevitably, the seven fliers are detailed to prepare for the Big Mission. Out of the exciting air battles that ensue with the enemy, only Philip remains aloft until he, too, goes into a tailspin, coincidentally plummeting into the now-evacuated village. But Jeannie has remained behind and, possessing the uncanny eyesight capable of following Phillip's every move in the skies high above, she also witnesses the crash. An ambulance takes him to the nearest hospital, but when Jeannie makes her way there to visit him, she's told that he has died of his wounds. Devastated, she sends lilacs (their mutual love-flower) to Philip's room. As she disconsolately wanders off, the bandaged hero receives Jeannie's bouquet, realizes that she must be near and drags himself to the window, from which he calls to her. And, finally, there's a happy ending.

But this smiling-through-tears finale is a long time coming, and *Lilac Time*'s audience cannot help but feel somewhat manipulated after so lengthy an unfoldment of this sentimental romance. On the plus side, the performances are excellent, and the enchanting Colleen Moore virtually puts this movie in her pocket. From wistful, clowning farmgirl to despondent tragedienne, she never for a moment ceases to convince and charm her audience.

THE SINGING FOOL

1928

CREDITS

A Warner Bros.-Vitaphone Picture. Directed by Lloyd Bacon. Screenplay by C. Graham Baker and Joseph Jackson. Based on the story by Leslie S. Barrows. Photographed by Byron Haskin. Edited by Ralph Dawson and Harold McCord. Songs: "Sonny Boy," "It All Depends on You" and "I'm Sittin' on Top of the World" by Lew Brown, B. G. DeSylva and Ray Henderson; "There's a Rainbow Round My Shoulder," "Keep Smiling at Trouble," "Golden Gate" and "Spaniard Who Blighted My Life" by Billy Rose, Al Jolson and Dave Dreyer. Music arranged by Louis Silvers. Sound by Vitaphone. Eleven reels.

CAST

Al Jolson (*Al Stone*); Betty Bronson (*Grace*); Josephine Dunn (*Molly Winton*); Reed Howes (*John Perry*); Edward Martindel (*Louis Marcus*); Arthur Housman (*Blackie Joe*); Davey Lee (*Sonny Boy*); Robert Emmett O'Connor (*Cafe Manager*).

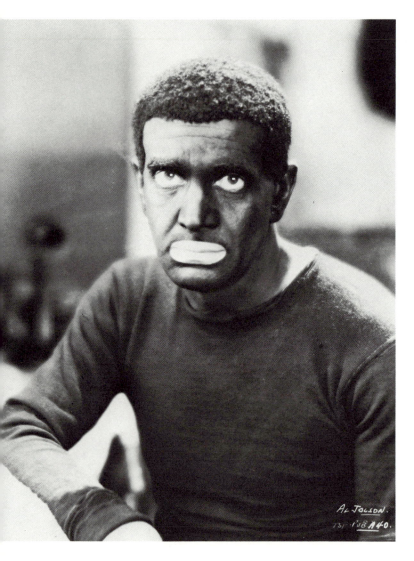

Al Jolson

The Jazz Singer, that legendary Al Jolson film hit of 1927, wasn't, of course, an *all*-talking film, demonstrating its use of sound only in musical numbers and brief bits of dialogue. But it caused the anticipated sensation among audiences, helped revolutionize the industry, tolled the death knell for any number of silent-screen careers and made a lot of money. But it was Jolson's follow-up, all-sound *The Singing Fool* a year later that really filled the Warner Bros. coffers, earning a then-astounding five and a half million dollars, which established a record unchallenged until a decade later, when *Gone With the Wind* became the box-office champ.

The Singing Fool came out at a time when the initial excitement over talking pictures had begun to wane, due largely to unperfected recording techniques and the static, stage-bound quality imposed on actors by the lack of microphone mobility. But the Jolson voice, via radio, recordings and stage appearances, was then immensely popular, and the attraction of an all-talking, all-singing musical comedy-drama starring that unabashedly tal-

Betty Bronson, Reed Howes, Josephine Dunn and Al Jolson

ented egotist was sufficient to make *The Singing Fool* 1928's runaway movie hit.

Jolson plays a singing waiter named Al Stone, who becomes a Broadway star by writing a hit song, enabling him to win as his wife Molly (Josephine Dunn), the chilly golddigger he covets. But Molly runs off with racketeer John Perry (Reed Howes, an actor best recalled as a Twenties Arrow Shirt model), taking with her their child, Sonny Boy (Davey Lee). Al falls on hard times, but cigarette girl Grace (Betty Bronson) sticks by him and inspires his comeback. And, in the film's four-hand-kerchief finale, Al goes from his little boy's deathbed to the stage, where the show goes on with Jolson's black-face number "Sonny Boy."

The Singing Fool's fame has, through the years, been oddly eclipsed by the now more accessible *The Jazz Singer*, a movie with which even some film historians have confused it! But it certainly represents the peak of Al Jolson's somewhat odd film career, despite the fact that he's out-acted by Davey Lee, the three-and-a-half-year-old who portrayed his doomed son. For *The Singing*

Fool's director, Lloyd Bacon, it was also an occasion, marking his first important assignment after five years turning out shorts and a few minor features. Just a few years hence, Bacon would be responsible for the direction of two of Warners' best musicals of the early Thirties, *42nd Street* and *Footlight Parade*.

Josephine Dunn and Al Jolson

Al Jolson (center)

Richard Arlen

BEGGARS OF LIFE

1928

CREDITS

A Paramount Picture. Presented by Adolph Zukor and Jesse L. Lasky. Produced and Directed by William A. Wellman. Assistant Director: Charles Barton. Scenario by Benjamin Glazer and Jim Tully, based on Tully's novel. Titles by Julian Johnson. Photographed by Henry Gerrard. Edited by Alyson Shaffer. Talking sequences, music score and sound effects by Movietone. Nine reels.

CAST

Wallace Beery (*Oklahoma Red*); Louise Brooks (*The Girl/Nancy*); Richard Arlen (*The Boy/Jim*); Edgar "Blue" Washington (*Black Mose*); H. A. Morgan (*Skinny*); Andy Clark (*Skelly*); Mike Donlin (*Bill*); Roscoe Karns (*Hopper*); Robert Perry (*The Arkansas Snake*); Johnnie Morris (*Rubin*); George Kotsonaros (*Baldy*); Jacques "Jack" Chapin (*Ukie*); Robert Brower (*Blind Sims*); Frank Brownlee (*Farmer*); Guinn "Big Boy" Williams (*Bakery Cart Driver*); Harvey Parry (*Hobo*).

This strikingly offbeat William Wellman picture about pre-Depression hoboes—one of them a girl disguised as a boy—anticipates not only Wellman's own *Wild Boys of the Road* (1933), but also Preston Sturges's excellent serio-comic *Sullivan's Travels* (1941). *Beggars of Life*, pigeon-holed by one contemporary critic as "a man's picture," seems a definite "find" to film historians viewing it today. But in 1928 it wasn't particularly well received, perhaps because of the grim realism with which it was shot—on location in the ruggedly rural and mountainous vicinity of Jacumba, California, near the Mexican border.

The movie's script was loosely based on a 1924 novel about life on the road by the "hobo writer" Jim Tully, who collaborated with Benjamin Glazer on its adaptation. The focus is on Jim (Richard Arlen), a young gentleman hobo who happens on the scene of a crime when he stops at a farmhouse to ask for breakfast. There he meets a frightened girl named Nancy (Louise Brooks), who has just shot and killed her adoptive father when he tried to rape her (Nancy's account of the incident unfolds interestingly in a quick succession of flashbacks superimposed over Brooks's face).

Louise Brooks

*Wallace Beery, Richard Arlen and
Louise Brooks*

Richard Arlen and Louise Brooks

Louise Brooks and Richard Arlen

Jim sympathizes with Nancy's plight, and he suggests that she accompany him, dressed in male attire, in search of a freight train to hop. This they manage, but they're tossed off by a brakeman and, after passing the night in a farmer's haystack, they find refuge in a "hobo jungle." There, a contest of wills takes place for leadership between Oklahoma Red (Wallace Beery) and Arkansas Snake (Robert Perry), and when detectives looking for Nancy disrupt the encampment, she and Jim hide out with Black Mose (Edgar "Blue" Washington) and a desperately ailing tramp in an abandoned cabin.

Red, who had earlier harbored an interest in Nancy, realizes that the girl loves Jim, and he helps them escape by bringing them a stolen car and female clothing for Nancy. The young couple drive away and, when the sick tramp dies, Red dresses the body in Nancy's discarded "drag" and situates him on a moving train's lumber car, which he then sets afire. But Red is shot down by detectives as he attempts to escape, and—as Jim and Nancy are seen riding atop a Canada-bound freight train—the self-sacrificing Red expires in a final close-up.

Fine direction by William Wellman reflects his ease with naturalistic subject matter like this, a virtual "vacation job" after the logistical problems of directing 1927's *Wings*. He also managed to draw some of their best-ever performances from his *Wings* star Arlen as well as burly character actor Beery and the hauntingly lovely Louise Brooks—whose natural beauty is scarcely enhanced by her costuming here. The actress has revealed that making this movie was less than a congenial experience, since Wellman looked down upon her as a dilettante, in addition to which she and Arlen harbored only thinly veiled contempt for one another. But none of this is evident on the screen, a factor which can only pay tribute to their performing skills.

Because Paramount wished to add sound to a part of this film, *Beggars of Life* was initially shown with Wallace Beery heard singing the song "Hark the Bells!" and spouting a bit of dialogue. But, on existing prints, that sound track is apparently now lost. *Beggars of Life*, however, remains a silent celluloid survivor and a late-Twenties tribute to Hollywood realism, enhanced by the artistry of its stars and director.

Norma Talmadge and Gustav von Seyffertitz.

THE WOMAN DISPUTED

1928

CREDITS

A United Artists Picture. Presented by Joseph M. Schenck. Directed by Henry King and Sam Taylor. Screenplay by C. Gardner Sullivan. Based on the play by Denison Clift. Photographed by Oliver Marsh. Edited by Hal Kern. Art Direction by William Cameron Menzies. Musical score by Hugo Riesenfeld. Song: "Woman Disputed, I Love You" by Bernie Grossman and Eddie Ward. Nine reels.

CAST

Norma Talmadge (*Mary Ann Wagner*); Gilbert Roland (*Paul Hartman*); Arnold Kent (*Nika Turgenov*); Boris De Fas (*The Passer-By*); Michael Vavitch (*Father Roche*); Gustav von Seyffertitz (*Otto Krueger*); Gladys Brockwell (*The Countess*); Nicholas Soussanin (*The Count*).

Norma Talmadge, Nicholas Soussanin, Gladys Brockwell and Gustav von Seyffertitz

Gilbert Roland and Norma Talmadge

From the viewpoint of the Eighties, it seems difficult to fathom a film career like that of Norma Talmadge, who was for years one of the silent screen's biggest stars. She entered motion pictures at the early age of thirteen, appearing in approximately 250 movies (mostly of the one- and two-reel variety) between 1910 and 1915. From 1915 to 1930, when she retired after two failed attempts at conquering the talking picture, Talmadge starred in fifty additional feature films. Thus, at age thirty-three, when many a current star has yet to reach her prime, this idol of the silent "photoplay" was already a multi-millionaire retiree with enough used celluloid in her filmography to equal the *lifetime* career of a Barbara Stanwyck.

The Woman Disputed, Norma's last silent picture, derived from Denison Clift's 1926 play, itself inspired by the classic Guy de Maupassant short story, *Boule de Suif*. On the stage, Ann Harding had starred in this World War I romantic melodrama about a noble-hearted Austrian prostitute who's courted by two officers, an Austrian (Gilbert Roland) and a Russian (Arnold Kent), whom she spurns for the former. Later, when the Russian troops capture her town and hold captive many of its leading citizens, our heroine surrenders herself to the Russian officer in exchange for the captives' freedom.

Although the very capable Henry King directed this film in its entirety, studio dissatisfaction with the results apparently caused Sam Taylor to be enlisted for additional shooting of a few climactic scenes, all of which appear negligible in the finished product. At thirty-one, Norma Talmadge was still at the height of her beauty. Playing opposite the lady was her offscreen man-of-the-moment—and previous team-mate from *Camille* (1927) and *The Dove* (1928)—Gilbert Roland. In an effort to keep *The Woman Disputed* consistent with then-current movie trends, it was released in two separate versions, one silent and the other accompanied by music and sound effects. But nothing could help its sluggish and dated narrative. Norma would go on to star, with her inappropriate Brooklyn accent, in a pair of early talkies that spelled the death of her once-great career: the static backstage-triangle drama *New York Nights* (1929), and an awkward costumer, *Du Barry, Woman of Passion* (1930). It was an untimely finale for a star who, less than a decade earlier, had drawn huge crowds to such successful Talmadge vehicles as *Smilin' Through* (1922), *Ashes of Vengeance* (1923) and *The Voice From the Minaret* (1923).

NOAH'S ARK

1928

Dolores Costello and George O'Brien

Myrna Loy and Dolores Costello.

George O'Brien and Dolores Costello

CREDITS

A Warner Bros. Picture. Produced by Darryl F. Zanuck. Directed by Michael Curtiz. Screenplay by Anthony Coldeway. Titles by De Leon Anthony. Story by Darryl F. Zanuck. Photographed by Hal Mohr and Barney McGill. Edited by Harold McCord. Miniature Effects by Fred Jackman. Musical score and synchronization by Louis Silvers. Talking sequences by Vitaphone. Song: "Heart o' Mine" by Billy Rose and Louis Silvers. Eleven reels.

CAST

Dolores Costello (*Mary/Miriam*); George O'Brien (*Travis/Japhet*); Noah Beery (*Nickoloff/King Nephilim*); Louise Fazenda (*Hilda/Tavern Maid*); Guinn "Big Boy" Williams (*Al/Ham*); Paul McAllister (*Minister/Noah*); Nigel de Brulier (*Soldier/High Priest*); Anders Randolf (*The German/Leader of Soldiers*); Armand Kaliz (*The Frenchman/Leader of the King's Guard*); Myrna Loy (*Dancer/Slave Girl*); William V. Mong (*The Innkeeper/Guard*); Malcolm Waite (*The Balkan/Shem*); Noble Johnson (*Broker*); Otto Hoffman (*Trader*); Joe Bonomo (*Aide to Leader of Soldiers*).

Dolores Costello (*center*)

Noah's Ark was one of Warner Bros.' most ambitious and expensive motion pictures of the late Twenties, running a lengthy (for those days) two hours and fifteen minutes. This may surprise those who know the movie only in its seventy-five-minute, bowdlerized version, as revamped by producer Robert Youngson for re-release in 1957. Originally a part-talkie, it was, oddly enough, those talking sequences, in addition to the intertitles, that Youngson eliminated. Thus the Fifties' Noah's Ark was, in essence, a silent film (as far as dialogue was concerned), with narration filling in the gaps caused by re-editing. As a result, the film now exists in a form so altered that it runs only seventy-five minutes—minus a full hour of the original footage! Probably, this is an improvement; and, of course, the film's raison d'être—the cataclysmic flood sequence—is still there.

Noah's Ark was conceived, like Cecil B. DeMille's Manslaughter (1922) and The Ten Commandments (1923), in a split-story form, paralleling a modern narrative with an ancient one. In the case of Noah's Ark—which likened man's sin and salvation of yore with his amorality in the Teens—that famed Biblical tale lies sandwiched between a framing account of the World War I romance between an Alsatian showgirl named Mary (Dolores Costello) and Travis (George O'Brien), an American. Both actors also play corresponding roles as lovers in the ancient portion, he being one of the sons of Noah, thus insuring them of a place on the Ark.

The movie's Budapest-born director Michael Curtiz had been brought to the U.S. in 1926 by the brothers Warner, for whom Noah's Ark was a big hit. Curtiz's later reputation for dictatorial treatment of actors and crew members alike has been substantiated by Noah's Ark's chief cameraman Hal Mohr, who left the film prior to its completion because of a violent disagreement with the director over the latter's handling of the flood and its destruction of some massive sets. Mohr knew this would endanger the lives of both stuntmen and extras, and suggested precautions that Curtiz refused to accept, allowing as how those parties would simply "have to take their chances." As a result, several extras were reportedly drowned. Not that the tragedy upset Curtiz's career. Before retiring in 1961, he went on to direct a total of eighty-eight films for Warner Bros.

THE WIND

1928

Lillian Gish

William Orlamond and Lillian Gish.

CREDITS

A Metro-Goldwyn-Mayer Picture. Directed by Victor Sea-strom. Scenario by Frances Marion. Titles by John Colton. Based on the novel by Dorothy Scarborough. Photographed by John Arnold. Art Direction by Cedric Gibbons and Edward Withers. Edited by Conrad A. Nervig. Costumes by Andre-ani. Theme song: "Love Brought the Sunshine" by Herman Ruby, William Axt, Dave Dreyer and David Mendoza. Sound effects by Movietone. Eight reels.

CAST

Lillian Gish (*Letty*); Lars Hanson (*Lige*); Montague Love (*Roddy*); Dorothy Cumming (*Cora*); Edward Earle (*Beverly*); William Orlamond (*Sourdough*); Laon Ramon, Carmencita Johnson and Billy Kent Schaefer (*Cora's Children*).

Dorothy Cumming and Lillian Gish.

Lillian Gish's memorable silent-screen career is peppered with film titles that are timeless classics of motion picture history: *The Birth of a Nation* (1915); *Intolerance* (1916); *True Heart Susie* (1919); *Way Down East* (1920); *Orphans of the Storm* (1921); *La Boheme* (1926); *The Scarlet Letter* (1926); and, marking the end of her silent career, *The Wind* (1928). Her beauty and talent were undeniable, but in the late Twenties, Gish's vehicles (over which the lady maintained tight control), while of high quality and garnering some excellent critical notices, failed to attract audiences. Of her two 1928 movies, *The Enemy* is among the lost curiosities of the period, while *The Wind* is an acknowledged classic. Upon release, however, the latter's stark realism and almost unrelieved gloom proved depressing, despite MGM's insistence on a happy ending. *Harrison's Reports*' hard-to-please critic called it "gruesome" and "irritating to the nerves." And, admittedly, the naturalistic handling of its prolonged desert wind-and-sand storm continue to have a marked effect on the film's audiences.

Gish plays a poor Virginia girl named Letty who's trainbound for her cousin's ranch in the desolate Western prairies, a region she ignorantly describes as "beautiful" to Roddy (Montague Love), a friendly stranger she meets en route. But Letty's stay is cut short when her cousin's wife Cora (Dorothy Cumming) grows jealous of the girl's closeness with her husband and three children. With no

Lillian Gish, William Orlamond and Lars Hanson.

Lillian Gish

Lillian Gish, Montague Love, Lars Hanson

place to go, Letty accepts Roddy's marriage invitation, only to find him already wed. Whereupon, she finds a legitimate husband in Lige (Lars Hanson), an uncouth man of the soil. But Roddy persists in his pursuit of her and, while Lige is away from home on a round-up, Roddy forces his attentions upon Letty, who shoots him in self-defense. What follows is a nightmare for the girl: in a fierce windstorm, she drags Roddy's body from the cabin and attempts to bury it in the sand. But the wind continually uncovers the body and, left alone to witness this gruesome spectacle from her window, Letty nearly goes mad.

Gish and her director, Victor Seastrom, wanted the movie's ending to follow that of the Dorothy Scarborough novel: driven insane, Letty wanders off into the storm. But MGM officials wouldn't hear of it; the public, they insisted, would never accept so downbeat a tragedy. And so, in the film's climax, Lige returns to Letty, bringing her the strength to face the desert elements.

But *The Wind* held little appeal for 1928's audiences and, like most of the other Gish vehicles of those years, it failed at the box-office. Meeting failure yet again with her talkie bow in *One Romantic Night* (1930), Lillian Gish went on to find greater favor with Broadway audiences as a Thirties stage actress.

THE BARKER

1928

Betty Compson and Milton Sills

CREDITS

A First National Picture. Presented by Richard A. Rowland. Produced by Al Rockett. Directed by George Fitzmaurice. Screenplay by Benjamin Glazer and Joseph Jackson. Titles by Herman J. Mankiewicz. Based on the play by Kenyon Nicholson. Photographed by Lee Garmes. Edited by Stuart Heisler. Costumes by Max Ree. Musical score by Louis Silvers. Sound by Vitaphone. Eight reels.

CAST

Milton Sills (*Nifty Miller*); Dorothy Mackaill (*Lou*); Betty Compson (*Carrie*); Douglas Fairbanks, Jr. (*Chris Miller*); Sylvia Ashton (*Ma Benson*); George Cooper (*Hap Spissel*); S. S. Simon (*Colonel Gowdy*); John Erwin (*Sailor West*).

By late 1928, the burgeoning sound revolution was creating havoc in motion pictures. Movies filmed silent were either being released "as is" for fast play-off to theatres not yet wired for talkies, or else their producers were adding music and sound effects. For those more ambitious, some silent features were being released with talking *sequences*. Soon many pictures would be made available in both silent and all-talking versions, while the nation's cinema owners struggled to install the requisite equipment.

The Barker was made as a silent—and apparently well-received at preview showings—but First National decided to inject sound effects, music and four talking sequences totaling some thirty-eight minutes of spoken dialogue. At other times, the usual intertitles were employed. Unfortunately, the sound engineering wasn't very good, and although the movie's quartet of stars all had stage-trained voices, their efforts were frequently muffled. As Mordaunt Hall wrote in his *New York Times* notice, "It was a relief when the scenes were silent."

Kenyon Nicholson's colorful stage drama of carnival life opened early in 1927 and ran for 225 Broadway performances with Walter Huston, Claudette Colbert and Norman Foster scoring in the leading roles. But, when it came to the movie version, Huston was unavailable and Colbert, who had made her film debut in *For the Love of Mike* (1927), was adjudged not sufficiently photogenic or enough of a "name." Consequently, their roles were recast by First National with tried-and-true film stars Milton Sills and Dorothy Mackaill, while Betty Compson and eighteen-year-old Douglas Fairbanks, Jr., took on the other two important roles.

As a movie, *The Barker* was forced to tone down some of the play's more authentic-sounding stage language (playwright Nicholson had joined an actual carnival to absorb background realism) and sexual implications. Nevertheless, it was a well-received movie that impressed the critics with its adult story of Nifty Miller (Sills), top-notch carnival barker who, seeking a better life for his son Chris (Fairbanks), packs him off to law school. But, during a summer vacation, the boy takes on a carnival job, thus complicating Nifty's live-in relationship with hula-dancer Carrie (Compson). Resenting Chris's presence with the sideshow, she pays Lou (Mackaill), another experienced carny gal, to seduce the innocent lad. But Chris and Lou fall genuinely in love, and their announced wedding plans send Nifty into a tailspin; he quits the show and takes to the bottle. But Lou's influence sends Chris back to law school, and Nifty returns to become a partner in the carnival.

The Barker marked silent star Betty Compson's talking-picture debut and impressed her peers sufficiently to bring her an Academy Award nomination as Best Actress of the 1928–1929 season. But Mary Pickford's *Coquette* took home the statuette.

In 1932, Fox remade *The Barker* with Clara Bow, Preston Foster, Richard Cromwell and Minna Gombell, and retitled it *Hoopla*. But it wasn't successful, and its poor reception marked Bow's retirement from the screen.

Douglas Fairbanks Jr. and Dorothy Mackaill

Douglas Fairbanks Jr., Dorothy Mackaill and Betty Compson.

A WOMAN OF AFFAIRS

1928   *Greta Garbo and John Gilbert*

CREDITS

A Metro-Goldwyn-Mayer Picture. Directed by Clarence Brown. Assistant Director: Charles Dorian. Scenario by Bess Meredyth. Titles by Marian Ainslee and Ruth Cummings. Based on Michael Arlen's novel *The Green Hat*. Photographed by William Daniels. Edited by Hugh Wynn. Art Direction by Cedric Gibbons. Costumes by Adrian. Song: "Love's First Kiss" by William Axt and David Mendoza. Sound effects and musical score by Movietone. Ten reels.

CAST

Greta Garbo (*Diana Merrick*); John Gilbert (*Neville Holderness*); Lewis Stone (*Dr. Hugh Trevelyan*); John Mack Brown (*David Furness*); Douglas Fairbanks, Jr. (*Jeffry Merrick*); Hobart Bosworth (*Sir Morton Holderness*); Dorothy Sebastian (*Constance*).

A Woman of Affairs is surely the quintessential silent Garbo picture. With her tall, willowy figure wrapped in Adrian's modish late-Twenties frocks, and her resolutely unshingled hair frequently sheathed in a cloche hat, she moves inevitably through this whitewashed, name-changed adaptation of Michael Arlen's sensational best-seller *The Green Hat* like a fascinating butterfly, laying waste the happiness (if not the very lives) of nearly every man (and at least one of their wives) in her fascinating orbit.

Diana Merrick (Garbo) and her tall, handsome wastrel of a brother Jeffry (Douglas Fairbanks, Jr.) have apparently abandoned their young British lives to the pursuit of irresponsible pleasures, carrying with them the reputation of fast living and independent morals. Most disapproving of their careless life style is the aristrocratic Sir Morton Holderness (Hobart Bosworth), with whose son Neville (John Gilbert) Diana is in love. Jeffry's only evident vice appears to be an affection for the bottle, for we never see him with a woman other than his sister (in Michael Arlen's version, she was his *twin*). Diana and Neville plan to elope, but his father nips this in the bud by lecturing the young man on family responsibility, and packs him off to Egypt on a diplomatic mission, before confronting a shocked Diana with this news. She, in turn, forces Sir Morton to admit that he deliberately sabotaged their romance. When he assures her that she will fall in love again, Diana counters fatalistically, "How little you know of love—my kind of love."

Diana then embarks on a reckless round of men,

Lewis Stone and Greta Garbo

Hobart Bosworth, John Gilbert and Greta Garbo

221

Douglas Fairbanks Jr., Greta Garbo and John Gilbert

Greta Garbo and John Mack Brown

parties and high life that we only learn about from the intertitles, before suddenly marrying Jeffry's best friend, David Furness (John Mack Brown), an embezzler who, tracked by the authorities, commits suicide on his honeymoon by leaping from his hotel window. It's a tragedy that Jeffry never forgives Diana for, sinking deeper into alcoholism and eventually expiring of it (from what little information we are given, we can only surmise that his feeling for Furness was a closet case).

Time passes and Neville turns up with a darkly attractive fiancée named Constance (Dorothy Sebastian), who soon realizes that she has competition for his deeper affections in the "legendary creature" now known as Diana Furness, who apparently has earned a wide-spread "reputation," with only her steadfast old friend Hugh (reliable old Lewis Stone, who would be Garbo's *husband* in her next vehicle, *Wild Orchids*) to fall back on.

Diana suffers a nervous breakdown and is hospitalized. Neville is so informed by Hugh, and he sends a huge bouquet of long-stemmed roses. But they're taken from her room for reasons of health, and when Diana awakens to find them gone, she deliriously wanders into the corridor to find them envased on a table. And, in the movie's most compelling scene, she fails to see the waiting Hugh, Neville and Constance as she crushes the flowers into her arms like a lover, murmuring to them, "I woke up—and you weren't there." Here, Garbo's intensely moving acting transcends all of her Hollywood work to that date. And we realize that our only reason for watching this somewhat confused and open-ended narrative is—Greta Garbo.

By this time, the film is nearly over. It's obvious that Neville still loves only Diana, and she him, a situation of which the not-so-dumb Constance is only too well aware, though she tries not to reveal it. And, for the last time, Diana proves that she is the "gallant lady" that the film's opening titles told us she was all along by sending Neville back to Constance and deliberately driving her car into the great oak tree that had always symbolized their love.

John Gilbert, Garbo's former lover, both onscreen (*Flesh and the Devil, Love*) and reportedly off, has little to do in *A Woman of Affairs*, for the script allows him no intelligent displays of either masculinity or nobility. In their cinematic relationship here, she appears always to take the upper hand, and his behavior, in the light of what the script tells us is an undying love, is difficult to fathom. Douglas Fairbanks, Jr., on the other hand, plays with all the flamboyant passion that Gilbert lacks. One believes in his announced decision to drink himself to death, although the storyline gives us no real indication as to his motives. Garbo's characterization, however, is completely enthralling, her fate preordained. We know we're accompanying her on a joyride to doom, and we take masochistic enjoyment in every phase of the journey. This is the magic of the actress and the icon named Garbo. Her expressive face tells us all that we need to know about Diana Merrick Furness; we don't need to hear her voice.

Douglas Fairbanks Jr. and Greta Garbo

Clarence Brown, who had previously directed Garbo and Gilbert in their sensational 1927 hit, *Flesh and the Devil*, again did the honors here, making as much as he could of a scenario that couldn't both be true to the book and appease the ever-vigilant Will Hays. And it is to Brown's credit that, in *A Woman of Affairs*, so much "unacceptable" material is made quite palatable indeed. Two years later, Garbo evinced enough faith in Brown to have him direct her belated but successful talkie debut in 1930's *Anna Christie*.

(Above), Greta Garbo, John Gilbert, Lewis Stone, Douglas Fairbanks Jr. and Hobart Bosworth

John Gilbert, Dorothy Sebastian and Greta Garbo.

THE BROADWAY MELODY

1929

CREDITS

A Metro-Goldwyn-Mayer Picture. Produced by Harry Rapf. Directed by Harry Beaumont. Ensemble numbers staged by George Cunningham. Scenario by Sarah Y. Mason. Dialogue by Norman Houston and James Gleason. Titles (for silent version) by Earl Baldwin. Original story by Edmund Goulding. Photographed by John Arnold. Color sequences by Technicolor. Editor of silent version: William Le Vanway. Edited by Sam S. Zimbalist. Art Direction by Cedric Gibbons. Costumes by David Cox. Songs: "The Wedding of the Painted Doll," "Broadway Melody," "Love Boat," "Boy Friend," and "You Were Meant for Me" by Nacio Herb Brown and Arthur Freed; "Give My Regards to Broadway" by George M. Cohan; "Truthful Deacon Brown" by Willard Robison. Sound Recording Engineer: Douglas Shearer. Sound Technicians: Wesley Miller, Louis Kolb, O. O. Ceccarini and G. A. Burns. Ten reels.

CAST

Anita Page (*Queenie Mahoney*); Bessie Love (*"Hank" Mahoney*); Charles King (*Eddie Kerns*); Jed Prouty (*Uncle Bernie*); Kenneth Thomson (*Jock*); Edward Dillon (*Stage Manager*); Mary Doran (*Blonde*); Eddie Kane (*Francis Zanfield*); J. Emmett Beck (*Babe Hatrick*); Marshall Ruth (*Stew*); Drew Demarest (*Turpe*); James Gleason (*Music Publisher*).

Anita Page and Bessie Love

Once the Hollywood studios began to accept the handwriting on the "sound" wall and realized that talking pictures were here to stay, they reasoned that if movies could talk they could also sing and dance. And as sound equipment rapidly improved, so motion pictures left the courtroom sets and moved backstage.

Metro-Goldwyn-Mayer really hit paydirt with its pioneering all-talking-singing-dancing musical *The Broadway Melody*, whose timing was so good that it scored all manner of "firsts." In the second year of the Academy Awards, *The Broadway Melody* was named Best Picture of 1928–29, over such diverse competition as United Artists' melodrama *Alibi*, Fox's Western *In Old Arizona*, Paramount's silent costume drama *The Patriot*, and Metro's other big musical of that season *The Hollywood Revue of 1929*.

The Broadway Melody was also Hollywood's first *original* movie musical, the first *talking* picture to receive the Academy Award, the first *musical* to be so honored, and *MGM*'s first Best Picture statuette. And among the Academy also-rans were *Broadway Melody* nominees Bessie Love (Best Actress) and Harry Beaumont (Best

Anita Page, Bessie Love and Charles King

Bessie Love, Charles King and Anita Page

Director). Because it was released at the start of 1929, before many of the nation's smaller theatres were equipped for sound, *The Broadway Melody* was also released in a silent version. And what a disappointment *that* must have been to sit through! For some years, the black-and-white films had had color sequences, and this one was no exception; its big "Wedding of the Painted Doll" production number was shot in Technicolor—the primitive sort of Technicolor where everything is either green or red.

To recount the movie's typical backstage plot, vaudeville hoofer Eddie Kerns (Charles King) writes a catchy song and is signed by Broadway-musical producer Francis Zanfield (Eddie Kane) to perform in one of his shows. Eddie persuades his long-time girlfriend "Hank" Mahoney (Bessie Love) to leave her current show and accompany him to New York with her sister Queenie (Anita Page), who's also her partner in a vaudeville act. When Eddie begins making a play for Queenie, she becomes the mistress of one of Zanfield's backers so that she won't be the cause of her sister's breaking up with Eddie. But Hank finds out that Eddie and Queenie love each other, and she gets him to take Queenie away from her protector. While her sister and Eddie resume their romance (likely to result in a very short-lived marriage), Hank recruits a new "sister" and returns to circuit vaudeville.

The songs, most of which were by the team of Arthur Freed and Nacio Herb Brown, had to be recorded "live" in those days—right there on the set, with an orchestra situated just beyond view of the camera. The movable boom-mike was yet to come, but director Harry Beaumont resourcefully improvised, placing the enclosed camera on wheels, while his sound technicians followed the performers quietly about in stocking-feet, holding out the microphones as needed. None of which made *The Broadway Melody* visually mobile. The movie was shot in a month's time at a cost of between $280,000 and $350,000. By the end of 1929, it had earned MGM a million dollars, and eventually the film grossed four million—mainly from theatres whose admission price was just thirty-five cents a head!

"The Wedding of the Painted Doll" production number

Rin-Tin-Tin

THE MILLION DOLLAR COLLAR

1929

CREDITS

A Warner Bros. Picture. Directed by D. Ross Lederman. Screenplay by Robert Lord. Titles by James A. Starr. Photographed by Nelson Laraby. Edited by William Holmes. Talking sequences, sound effects and musical score by Vitaphone. Six reels.

CAST

Rin-Tin-Tin (*Rinty*); Matty Kemp (*Bill Holmes*); Evelyn Pierce (*Mary French*); Philo McCullough (*Joe French*); Tommy Dugan (*Ed Mack*); Allan Cavan (*The Chief*); Grover Liggon (*Scar*).

Long before a male collie ironically named Lassie became a big Forties box-office draw for Metro-Goldwyn-Mayer, there was Rin-Tin-Tin. In 1925, this handsome German Shepherd was Hollywood's biggest star, as well as the main audience attraction for his studio, Warner Bros. Beginning with 1922's *The Man from Hell River*, and continuing through the decade, this canine star maintained an unprecedented popularity, rivalled by the only-slightly-less-popular dog Strongheart. Rinty's billing usually came before the title of his movies, and most definitely ahead of his two-footed co-stars. Of all the silent stars threatened by the coming of sound, he was undoubtedly the least intimidated of all, barking his way through a number of early talkies prior to his death in 1932, at sixteen. In 1976, Hollywood's greatest animal star became the subject of a thinly-disguised satirical biofilm, *Won Ton Ton, the Dog Who Saved Hollywood*.

Rinty's best movies were of the silent period, usually with outdoor settings like *Where the North Begins* (1923), *The Lighthouse by the Sea* (1924) and *Clash of the Wolves* (1925). A number of his Twenties screenplays were written by a fledgeling Warner Bros. screenwriter named Darryl F. Zanuck, who had a knack for mixing the requisite ingredients of comedy, drama and adventure. Like many Germany Shepherds, Rin-Tin-Tin was not

Evelyn Pierce, Rin-Tin-Tin and Matty Kemp

particularly easy to work with and he enjoyed the dubious reputation of occasionally attacking his directors and fellow performers. But he was a most attractive scene-stealer and even quite a good actor, under the training of his owner and master, Captain Lee Duncan, who had discovered him as a puppy in a German trench during World War I.

The Million Dollar Collar, a standard crook melodrama and one of four movies in which Rinty appeared during 1929, was released in both silent and sound versions. Its plot revolved around the dog collar of the title, inside which jewel thieves had hidden a valuable necklace. A complex and contrived storyline hurtles the crook's robbery car into a lake, along with his dog. But a young tramp named Bill (the film's nominal hero, played by Matty Kemp) saves Rinty from a watery fate, dons his master's clothing and, coincidentally arrives at the lodge where the thief's accomplice (Philo McCullough, Rin-Tin-Tin's only rival for acting honors here) mistakes Bill for the drowned robber. The villain's pretty sister Mary (played by a long-forgotten starlet named Evelyn Pierce) plays up to Bill, in order to learn the whereabouts of the gems. Instead, she falls in love with him, while Rinty gets into the act as much as possible, and literally keeps them from getting together too soon. And, after a number of thrilling escapades, Rinty brings the forest rangers, the lovers are rescued and the gang is arrested.

D. Ross Lederman, who had guided his canine star through *A Dog of the Regiment* (1927) and *Rinty of the Desert* (1928) capably did the honors again here. The result was a standard program picture for Rinty's fans.

Matty Kemp and Rin-Tin-Tin.

THE LETTER

1929

Jeanne Eagels and Herbert Marshall

CREDITS

A Paramount Picture. Produced by Monta Bell. Directed by Jean de Limur. Screenplay by Garrett Fort, Jean de Limur and Monta Bell. Based on the play by Somerset Maugham. Photographed by George Folsey. Edited by Jean de Limur and Monta Bell. Six reels.

CAST

Jeanne Eagels (*Leslie Crosbie*); O. P. Heggie (*Mr. Joyce*); Reginald Owen (*Robert Crosbie*); Herbert Marshall (*Geoffrey Hammond*); Irene Brown (*Mrs. Joyce*); Lady Tsen Mei (*Li-Ti*); Tamaki Yoshiwara (*Ong Chi Seng*).

Reginald Owen and Jeanne Eagels

The restrictions of microphones in that early-talkie year of 1929 undoubtedly account for the sound-stage confinements that make *The Letter* look pretty much like a photographed stage play. Director Jean de Limur takes obvious pains to create an atmosphere of steamy courtrooms and Oriental alleyways but, as in the play, there is little action, with the story's interest centering on all the secrets, lies and revelations of character.

The Letter's by-now-familiar plot unfolds on an East Indian rubber plantation where the bored and restless Leslie Crosbie (played by Broadway favorite Jeanne Eagels) turns to another man (Herbert Marshall) for the attentions her husband (Reginald Owen) neglects to give her. But when her lover attempts to end their affair because of his liaison with a Chinese woman, Leslie shoots and kills him, precipitating a murder trial at which she convinces everyone that she only fired the gun in defense of her honor. Complications arise when the Oriental woman (Lady Tsen Mei) turns up a letter that Leslie wrote to her lover, urging him to visit her the night he was killed. To retrieve the incriminating evidence, Leslie must humiliate herself before her rival, who demands $10,000 for the letter. Acquitted of the crime, Leslie is forced to reveal the truth to her husband when he questions her lawyer's extra $10,000 charge. The story concludes with the couple bound together in loveless guilt.

The movie marked Paramount's first all-talking feature to be produced at its New York facilities in Astoria, a factor necessitated by the decision to cast working stage actors in the key roles. The result was a collection of seasoned performers with voices, of course, that recorded exceptionally well. But especially impressive was Jeanne

Jeanne Eagels and unidentified players

Jeanne Eagels.

Eagels, the legendary star of another highly dramatic, earlier Somerset Maugham story, *Rain*. Her climactic scene with Owen, in which she tells him the truth at last, admitting that she still loves the man she killed, remains a highly effective example of acting artistry. It also helped gain Eagels an Academy Award nomination. Gossip about her hectic private life helped sell *The Letter* to metropolitan audiences. But in the remainder of the country, where Eagels's name was unimportant, there was little Paramount could do to "sell" this picture, and it failed at the box-office. The actress only made one more

picture, 1929's *Jealousy*, before dying later that year, at the age of thirty-five, of a heroin overdose.

As a film, *The Letter* didn't enjoy success until 1940 when, at the height of her career, Bette Davis played it brilliantly under William Wyler's direction. Seven years later, as *The Unfaithful*, its altered plot served as a mediocre vehicle for Ann Sheridan. And more recently, with the advantage of the Eighties' sexual frankness, Lee Remick found *The Letter* an excellent TV-movie vehicle in 1982.

THE DIVINE LADY

1929

Corinne Griffith

H.B. Warner, Victor Varconi and Corinne Griffith

Corinne Griffith and Victor Varconi

CREDITS

A First National Picture. Presented by Richard A. Rowland. Associate Producer: Walter Morosco. Directed by Frank Lloyd. Scenario by Agnes Christine Johnston and Forrest Halsey. Titles by Harry Carr and Edwin Justus Mayer. Based on the novel *The Divine Lady; a Romance of Nelson and Emma Hamilton* by E. Barrington. Photographed by John F. Seitz. Edited by Hugh Bennett. Art Direction by Horace Jackson. Costumes by Max Ree. Sound sequences by Vitaphone. Song: "Lady Divine" by Joseph Pasternak and Richard Kountz. Twelve reels.

CAST

Corinne Griffith (*Emma Hart, Lady Hamilton*); Victor Varconi (*Captain Horatio Nelson*); H. B. Warner (*Sir William Hamilton*); Ian Keith (*Charles Greville*); Marie Dressler (*Mrs. Hart*); Dorothy Cumming (*Queen of Naples*); William Conklin (*George Romney*); Montagu Love (*Captain Hardy*); Julia Swayne Gordon (*Duchess of Argyle*); Helen Jerome Eddy (*Lady Nelson*); Michael Vavitch (*King of Naples*); Evelyn Hall (*Duchess of Devonshire*).

Corinne Griffith (1898–1979) was so strikingly beautiful that she was often referred to as the "Orchid Lady" of the screen. Indeed, like numerous others in Hollywood history, her beauty was sufficient unto her stardom, and she was seldom called upon to act. But Griffith's popularity was considerable in the Twenties, and her natural business acumen made her one of the silent era's biggest money-makers.

The Divine Lady, the movie for which Griffith is best remembered today, took some liberties with the much-filmed, adulterous story of Lord Nelson and Lady Hamilton that later served as a showcase for the talents of Laurence Olivier and Vivien Leigh (*That Hamilton Woman/Lady Hamilton*; 1941), and Peter Finch and Glenda Jackson (*Bequest to the Nation/The Nelson Affair*; 1973).

Basically a silent film, *The Divine Lady* had no dialogue. But it did utilize sound effects, as well as a song. Its production reflected the obvious care and expense that had gone into its making, with sumptuous sets, costumes and photography and remarkable care given to its shipboard battle sequences, enlivened by the audible thunder of big guns. Both the film's direction and acting were

Ian Keith and Corinne Griffith

accorded due praise. Unfortunately, this costume drama was planned and filmed as a silent, and released at a time (March, 1929) when talking pictures were becoming increasingly more popular. Worse still, Corinne Griffith's first talkie, the contemporary comedy-drama *Saturday's Children*, was released only two months after *The Divine Lady*—and by the same distributor, First National. And as a result, the latter's box-office receipts were somewhat disappointing.

In this, the second year of the Academy Awards, *The Divine Lady* came away with two statuettes, one for the photography of John F. Seitz (inventor of the matte shot, and known for his striking use of low-key lighting) and Frank Lloyd's direction. An interesting sidelight to the latter award: in contrast to more recent years, the 1928–29 competition listed seven films nominated for Best Direction, including no less than *three* (*Weary River*, *Drag* and *The Divine Lady*) directed by Frank Lloyd!

Norma Shearer

THE TRIAL OF MARY DUGAN

1929

CREDITS

A Metro-Goldwyn-Mayer Picture. Directed by Bayard Veiller. Screenplay by Becky Gardiner and Bayard Veiller, based on his stage play. Photographed by William Daniels. Edited by Blanche Sewell. Art Direction by Cedric Gibbons. Costumes by Adrian. Sound by Movietone. Recording Engineers: J. K. Brock and Douglas Shearer. Twelve reels.

CAST

Norma Shearer (*Mary Dugan*); Lewis Stone (*Edward West*); H. B. Warner (*District Attorney Galway*); Raymond Hackett (*Jimmy Dugan*); Lilyan Tashman (*Dagmar Lorne*); Olive Tell (*Mrs. Edgar Rice*); Adrienne D'Ambricourt (*Marie Ducrot*); DeWitt Jennings (*Police Inspector Hunt*); Wilfred North (*Judge Nash*); Landers Stevens (*Dr. Welcome*); Myra Hampton (*May Harris*); Westcott Clarke (*Police Captain Price*); Charles Moore (*James Madison*); Claud Allister (*Henry Plaisted*).

With the advent of the talking picture, and its attendant restrictions on action to accommodate the miking problems of 1928–29, it was thought expedient to explore the availability of good courtroom dramas that had already proven their strength in successful Broadway engagements. As a result, Warner Bros. came out first with a 1928 adaptation of Elmer Rice's play *On Trial* (a well-played but poorly recorded legal thriller), and MGM followed, in the spring of 1929, with *The Trial of Mary Dugan*. The latter, marking the speaking debut of Metro's top leading lady Norma Shearer, not only received critical kudos for its dramatic power, but also was unanimously acclaimed for the audible clarity of its sound, for which Norma's brother Douglas and J. K. Brock took the credit.

The Trial of Mary Dugan was written by Bayard Veiller, whose stage dramas *Within the Law* and *The Thirteenth Chair* were each successfully filmed more than once. In

1927, with Ann Harding as Mary in a cast that featured Arthur Hohl and Rex Cherryman, *The Trial of Mary Dugan* had run for a smash-hit 437 performances, making it an attractive prospect for Hollywood. Playwright Veiller, in the interests of protecting his brainchild, successfully negotiated with MGM, contracting not only to supervise Becky Gardiner's movie adaptation, but also to *direct* the work as well. The result, in twelve reels, runs close to two hours—a long film for 1929. But Veiller's guidance helps retain the integrity of his stage play and as much of its "adult" content as that pre-Production Code era would allow.

In essence, Broadway showgirl Mary Dugan (Shearer) is something of a high-class prostitute, having been the mistress of successive gentlemen—all so that she could finance the legal studies of her younger brother Jimmy (Raymond Hackett). When the most recent of her sugar-daddies, a wealthy playboy, is knifed to death, Mary is arrested and put on trial for his murder. Defending her is her old friend Edward West (Lewis Stone), who all but refuses to cross-examine his witness. The outrage thus exhibited by Jimmy Dugan, now fresh from law school, moves West suddenly to drop Mary's case. Whereupon, her brother, despite his lack of professional experience (the film's biggest plot drawback), resumes Mary's defense. Jimmy cannot keep his sister's sullied past from surfacing during the trial, but he finally manages to gain her acquittal by disclosing the killer—Edward West!

As a vehicle for Norma Shearer, *The Trial of Mary Dugan* is an interesting landmark, for her speaking voice pleased her multitude of fans with its pleasant modulations and cultured tones that, to her credit, lacked the pseudo-British phoniness of so many of Hollywood's recent *Broadway* emigrés. And the vocal economy of her role—Mary is much talked *about*, but doesn't *herself* speak until some thirty minutes into the film—was clever showmanship that helped, of course, to build dramatic tension and interest in her character.

Aside from a couple of brief "opening up" sequences, Veiller's film, like his stage play, remains within the confines of the courtroom. That set, the author revealed in his autobiography *The Fun I've Had*, was painted "on the thinnest kind of cheesecloth," since sound reflected from the canvas they would otherwise have used. Adding to the discomforts of *Mary Dugan*'s production, Veiller recalls, was the intensity of the lights. "We couldn't have any fans to let out the super-heated air—they made a

H.B. Warner and Norma Shearer

Lilyan Tashman, Norma Shearer, H.B. Warner,
unidentified players and Raymond Hackett

noise—so the temperature on the sound-stage in those days ran to about 120 or 130 degrees, and that's what we worked in."

Generally very well acted by its stellar names, the movie comes in for some expert comic scene-stealing by Lilyan Tashman's ditzy fellow-showgirl and, especially, Adrienne D'Ambricourt as a priceless French maid, who repeatedly misinterprets the D.A.'s questioning.

The Trial of Mary Dugan was remade in 1941, and proved a minor-starmaking vehicle for Laraine Day, who never quite managed to become another Norma Shearer.

Norma Shearer and Lewis Stone

MADAME X
(Absinthe)

Ullrich Haupt and Ruth Chatterton 1929

Lewis Stone and Ruth Chatterton

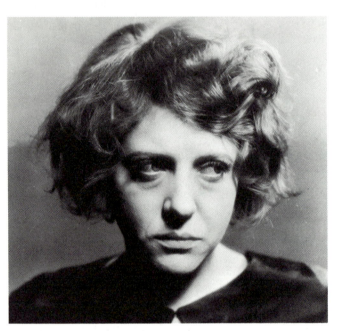

Ruth Chatterton

CREDITS

A Metro-Goldwyn-Mayer Picture. Directed by Lionel Barrymore. Screenplay by Willard Mack. Based on the play by Alexandre Bisson. Photographed by Arthur Reed. Edited by William S. Gray. Art Direction by Cedric Gibbons. Costumes by David Cox. Sound by Movietone. Recording Engineers: Russell Franks and Douglas Shearer. Ten reels.

CAST

Lewis Stone (*Floriot*); Ruth Chatterton (*Jacqueline*); Raymond Hackett (*Raymond Floriot*); Holmes Herbert (*Noel*); Eugenie Besserer (*Rose*); John P. Edington (*Doctor*); Mitchell Lewis (*Colonel Hanby*); Ullrich Haupt (*Laroque*); Sidney Toler (*Merivel*); Richard Carle (*Perissard*); Carroll Nye (*Darrell*); Claude King (*Valmorin*); Chappell Dossett (*Judge*); Mary Gordon (*Nursemaid*); Dickie Moore (*Little Boy*).

Alexandre Bisson's emotionally overwrought French tear-jerker opened on Broadway in 1910 and, to date, has reached the English-speaking screen five times, its popularity obviously due to its appeal to talented actresses capable of portraying the title role, and audiences seeking a sentimental wallow. Its Broadway star, Dorothy Donnelly, first filmed it in 1915; Pauline Frederick scored a great success in a 1920 film adaptation; Ruth Chatterton brought sound to the role in 1929; Gladys George impressed the critics in 1937, and—after a near-thirty-year gap—Lana Turner's artificial glamour in the 1966 movie's first half made all the more striking her impressive depiction of alcoholic degradation in the later scenes. Finally, Tuesday Weld essayed this tragic part in a slick 1981 TV-movie update.

But audience tastes have changed dramatically through the years, along with mores and morals, and *Madame X*'s reflections on sin and redemption, mother love and sacrifice have long since become hopelessly outdated. Today, a reevaluation of the 1929 movie is more amusing—for its overwrought, unabashedly sentimental melodramatics—than it is moving or tear-inducing. As the errant wife who leaves her lawyer-husband (Lewis Stone, who received top billing) and infant son to run off with a more exciting lover, Ruth Chatterton pulls out all the emotional stops in an acting style of excessive theatricality, especially in her grand but hysterical line readings during the early scene in which she returns to beg a stony Lewis Stone to let her visit their ailing child. Later, as Chatterton's character descends the social scale via absinthe addiction and association with the wrong kind of men, her performance improves tremendously, and her drunk scenes with the subtly villainous Ullrich Haupt can only represent 1929's screen-acting art at its finest. Chatterton even helps us believe *Madame X*'s incredible courtroom climax, blending sentiment, irony and coincidence beyond all logic. What was once considered heart-rending drama now seems like bathetic parody or perhaps a satiric skit from TV's *Saturday Night Live*.

But in a year uneasily adjusting to the fact that talking pictures were here to stay, the 1929 *Madame X*, directed by an indulgent Lionel Barrymore, appeared on several Ten Best lists. It also won Academy Award nominations—but no awards—for both Barrymore and Chatterton.

THE COCOANUTS

1929

Margaret Dumont and Groucho Marx

CREDITS

A Paramount Picture. Executive Producer: Monta Bell. Produced by Walter Wanger. Associate Producer: James R. Cowan. Directed by Robert Florey and Joseph Santley. Screenplay by Morrie Ryskind. Based on the stage musical by George S. Kaufman and Morrie Ryskind. Photographed by George Folsey. Edited by Barney Rogan. Music and lyrics by Irving Berlin. Song: "When My Dreams Come True." Musical direction by Frank Teurs. Sound by Movietone. Ten reels.

CAST

Groucho Marx (*Mr. Hammer*); Harpo Marx (*Harpo*); Chico Marx (*Chico*); Zeppo Marx (*Jamison*); Mary Eaton (*Polly Potter*); Oscar Shaw (*Bob*); Katherine (Kay) Francis (*Penelope*); Margaret Dumont (*Mrs. Potter*); Cyril Ring (*Harvey Yates*); Basil Ruysdael (*Hennessy*); Sylvan Lee (*Bell Captain*); with the Gamby-Hale Ballet Girls, and the Allan K. Foster Girls.

Although *The Cocoanuts* brought the wildly uninhibited nonsense humor of the Marx Brothers to the moviegoing public, it wasn't quite the team's initial encounter with filmmaking. Harpo had already done a brief solo stint in 1925's *Too Many Kisses* that was almost subliminal by the time the Paramount comedy's editors had finished with it. And, as a group, the brothers clowned their way through a silent 1926 short entitled *Humorisk* that was reportedly shown only once to the public, at a Bronx matinee. Groucho's explanation: "It wasn't very good." Supposedly, the movie was later destroyed.

Originally, the brothers had been five—a quintet of siblings born to Sam and Minnie Marx, starting in 1891, and subsequently stage-named Chico, Harpo, Groucho, Zeppo and Gummo. As an act, they began in vaudeville circa 1908, but it was some sixteen years before they reached the bigtime—as a quartet (Gummo had left the act)—in the Broadway show called *I'll Say She Is!* This hit

Zeppo Marx, Kay Francis, Mary Eaton, Groucho Marx, Oscar Shaw, Cyril Ring and Margaret Dumont

was, in turn, followed by *The Cocoanuts*, which scored an even greater success.

In 1929, while the brothers were performing on Broadway in *Animal Crackers* at night, their days were spent turning *The Cocoanuts* into a motion picture at Paramount's New York studios in Astoria. The early talking pictures looked to Broadway for exploitable talent, and the Marxes' then-current stage popularity made their appearance in films inevitable. As a movie, *The Cocoanuts* became less of a musical and more of a comedy than it had been on the stage—with the emphasis on the brothers, although too much footage was given over to the insipid romancing of ingenue leads Mary Eaton and Oscar Shaw. In more sophisticated roles were Cyril Ring and that statuesque lisper, Kay (but then still billed as "Katherine") Francis. But *The Cocoanuts'* best scenes are those with the Brothers and Margaret Dumont (who would serve as their perfect-dowager foil throughout the best years of their Hollywood classics) as they cope with a slim plot hinging on a Florida real-estate development scheme.

Today *The Cocoanuts* dates badly, with its nonsense prattle, antiquated jokes, dreadful puns and ethnic slurs. And there are the usual problems with the early sound recording equipment. Robert Florey, the movie's unenthusiastic director, has admitted that, since the free-wheeling Brothers were retreading material with which they were overly familiar from the stage, his job was mainly "directing traffic." He has also confessed to laughing so hard on the movie's set that he'd habitually ruin the sound track, and finally had to signal his directions from within a sound-proof glass booth.

OUR MODERN MAIDENS

1929

Joan Crawford

CREDITS

A Metro-Goldwyn-Mayer Picture. Directed by Jack Conway. Screenplay by Josephine Lovett. Titles by Marian Ainslee and Ruth Cummings. Photographed by Oliver Marsh. Edited by Sam S. Zimbalist. Art Direction by Cedric Gibbons. Gowns by Adrian. Musical score by William Axt. Dance Direction by George Cunningham. Music and sound effects by Movietone. Eight reels.

CAST

Joan Crawford (*Billie Brown*); Rod La Rocque (*Glenn Abbott*); Douglas Fairbanks, Jr. (*Gil Jordan*); Anita Page (*Kentucky*); Edward Nugent (*Reg*); Josephine Dunn (*Ginger*); Albert Gran (*B. Bickering Brown*).

Joan Crawford and Rod La Rocque

After four years as a featured player at Metro-Goldwyn-Mayer, the increasingly popular Joan Crawford finally became a star in this, her last silent picture. *Our Modern Maidens* was a follow-up to her big hit of 1928, the better-remembered *Our Dancing Daughters*. Like its predecessor, *Our Modern Maidens*, as written by scenarist Josephine Lovett, offered Jazz Age audiences an up-to-date tale of restless flappers and the rather cavalier manner in which they play with their boyfriends' emotions. Marriage doesn't mean very much in this foolish story of romantic mix-ups, but moral values aren't what this movie is about, anyway. MGM gambled successfully that, in the autumn of 1929, when most silent films were getting a quick playoff as remnants of a fast-dying breed, the nation's youth would still flock to a motion picture cast with attractive and popular players in a racy romantic plot that might then have been termed "hot stuff."

Offscreen, Crawford was keeping company with Douglas Fairbanks, Jr., and their official "engagement" had been publicly announced just prior to this film's production. So there was added interest in their screen teaming here. *Our Modern Maidens* cast them as Billie Brown and Gil Jordan, a young couple who plan to get married. He's studying to be a diplomat; she's a motor tycoon's fun-loving daughter. But, from that point on, the storyline turns unconventional. Prior to their wedding, Billie realizes that she's actually in love with Glenn Abbott (Rod La Rocque), the old friend she visits to help Gil get a diplomatic post. Gil, in turn, has too much to drink at a wild party and enjoys a pleasurable misadventure with a free-wheeling girl named Kentucky (Anita Page), which

Joan Crawford

Anita Page and Douglas Fairbanks Jr

Douglas Fairbanks Jr. and Joan Crawford

results in her pregnancy. Nevertheless, Billie and Gil, the unloving couple, go through with the wedding ceremony. But she eventually finds out about her groom's affair with Kentucky, and Billie leaves him to get an annulment in Paris. Later, Billie turns up in South America, where Abbott is an ambassador. At the fadeout, it appears that she will marry him, while Gil presumably makes an honest woman of the promiscuous Kentucky.

MGM decked this one out lavishly, from Adrian's modish wardrobe to the striking art-deco sets of Cedric Gibbons. And the reckless action is well paced by the capable but underrated Jack Conway, with whom Joan Crawford obviously felt very comfortable, since he had already directed her in a pair of 1927 Metro features, *Twelve Miles Out* and *The Understanding Heart*.

As an amusing sidelight of this production, it's interesting to note that an earlier version of the script brought the Crawford and Fairbanks characters *back together* for the finale. But MGM boss Louis B. Mayer objected: Crawford's fiancé was merely on loan from another studio, while Rod La Rocque was, like Joan, under contract to Metro. So there could be no question but that Leo the Lion's own must unite for the movie's fadeout. So much for the power of executive whim in those days of the studio contract system.

With Joan Crawford dancing, romancing and even suffering a bit, *Our Modern Maidens* could only be another hit for Metro, anticipating a third follow-up Crawford drama in 1930, the somewhat more sober but equally popular *Our Blushing Brides*.

Rod La Rocque and Joan Crawford

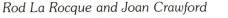

THE GREAT GABBO

1929

Erich von Stroheim and Otto

CREDITS

A Sono Art-World Wide Picture. A Henry D. Meyer-Nat Cordish Presentation. Directed by James Cruze. Screenplay by Hugh Herbert. Based on Ben Hecht's story *The Rival Dummy*. Photographed by Ira H. Morgan. Color sequences by Multicolor. Art Direction by Robert E. Lee. Costumes by Andre-ani. Dance numbers supervised by Maurice L. Kusell. Musical Direction by Howard Jackson. Songs: "The New Step," "I'm in Love With You," "I'm Laughing," "Ickey," "Every Now and Then," "The Web of Love" and "The Ga-Ga Bird" by Paul Titsworth, Lynn Cowan, Donald McNamee and King Zany. Ten reels.

CAST

Erich von Stroheim (*The Great Gabbo*); Betty Compson (*Mary*); Donald Douglas (*Frank*); Margie "Babe" Kane (*Babe*); Otto Gabbo (*Himself, a Dummy*).

Erich von Stroheim, Betty Compson and Otto

By 1929, the career of Erich von Stroheim was in an unfortunate state of flux. The direction of Gloria Swanson's expensive silent *Queen Kelly* had been taken away from him at her behest, and the unfinished picture shelved, to be shown only in Europe in a version patched together by Swanson herself. Consequently, producers were more inclined to hire Stroheim as an actor than as a director. At the same time, producer-director James Cruze (from 1918 through 1927 a mainstay at Paramount, where he first gained major recognition for 1923's *The Covered Wagon*) found his career on the wane with the coming of sound. Reportedly the highest paid director in the world in 1927, he had solidified his reputation with *Merton of the Movies* (1924), *Beggar on Horseback* (1925) and *Old Ironsides* (1926). But Cruze had begun his career as an actor and stuntman, and much of his best work was represented by films of action and visual appeal. In 1929, after two movies at Pathé and three for MGM, Cruze turned to independent production with *The Great Gabbo*. In this drama with music, Cruze cast his wife Betty Compson in the female lead of a vaudeville performer, and hired Stroheim to make his talking-picture acting bow as the arrogant, egotistical ventriloquist named Gabbo, whose alter ego is his lifelike dummy Otto. Compson plays Gabbo's browbeaten assistant Mary, who is probably his mistress as well. It's apparent that she adores Gabbo, but all of her service goes without

Otto, Betty Compson and Erich von Stroheim

gratitude, and finally she's dismissed from the act, after making a clumsy but minor mistake.

Time passes, and Gabbo goes on to greater fame and fortune with Otto, while Mary marries and forms a song-and-dance act with her husband Frank (Donald Douglas). Eventually, all find themselves performing on the same vaudeville stage, and Gabbo realizes, too late, how much he has always cared for Mary. Learning of her marriage, however, drives Gabbo over the brink of sanity, and he disrupts a performance, smashing his dummy and wandering from the theatre with Otto under his arm as he witnesses workmen taking down the sign advertising "The Great Gabbo."

This striking film has occasionally—and unfairly—been dismissed as a cheap poverty-row melodrama. More responsible reappraisal reveals a respectably well-made movie that doesn't really look cheap at all, especially in its several rather elaborate production numbers (originally shot in the Multicolor process). That these musical sequences offer a bit too much "padding" to offset the ventriloquist's story, demonstrates an apparent lack of

faith in Stroheim's ability to draw an audience on his own. And, although the cast is small (and several supporting players go totally without credit), the picture is well acted, especially by Stroheim and Betty Compson, both of whom won additional critical praise at the time for their well-modulated speaking voices.

The Great Gabbo's strength, of course, lies in Stroheim's admirable performance of a character that ranges from the despicable to the poignant. In one scene, he even makes us believe Gabbo's ability to make the dummy both talk and sing while his master is seated halfway across the room—consuming a leisurely meal.!

This Ben Hecht story's influence on future films is undeniable, for without *The Great Gabbo* there would not perhaps have been such later variations on the theme as the Michael Redgrave sequence in England's *Dead of Night* (1946) or Anthony Hopkins's under-appreciated tour-de-force in *Magic* (1978). In his 1983 biography of Stroheim, *The Man You Loved to Hate*, Richard Koszarski reveals that the actor once tried to acquire the rights to a remake, only to discover that ventriloquist Edgar Bergen had already done so.

APPLAUSE

1929

Helen Morgan

Fuller Mellish Jr. and Helen Morgan

Rouben Mamoulian directing Joan Peers and Helen Morgan

CREDITS

A Paramount Picture. Directed by Rouben Mamoulian. Produced by Jesse L. Lasky and Monta Bell. Screenplay by Garrett Fort. Based on the novel by Beth Brown. Photographed by George Folsey. Edited by John Bassler. Sound recording by Ernest F. Zatorsky. Songs: "What Wouldn't I Do for That Man?" by E. Y. Harburg and Jay Gorney; "Yaaka Hula Hickey Dula" by E. Ray Goetz, Joe Young and Pete Wendling; "Give Your Little Baby Lots of Lovin'" by Dolly Morse and Joe Burke; and "I've Got a Feelin' I'm Fallin'" by Billy Rose, Harry Link and "Fats" Waller. Nine reels.

CAST

Helen Morgan (*Kitty Darling*); Joan Peers (*April Darling*); Fuller Mellish, Jr. (*Hitch Nelson*); Henry Wadsworth (*Tony*); Jack Cameron (*Joe King*); Dorothy Cumming (*Mother Superior*).

With the advent of talking pictures, Hollywood producers went out of their way to court Broadway stage veterans, not only for starring roles in movies, but also as directors and dialogue coaches. Russian-born (and Moscow Art Theatre-trained) Rouben Mamoulian had justly earned his reputation as an inventive stylist of the theatre, and had staged, among others, the successful Theatre Guild productions of *Porgy* and *Marco Millions* when Paramount approached him to helm *Applause*, a film to be produced at their New York studios in Astoria. Before starting the assignment, Mamoulian closely studied the techniques of other directors filming at Astoria. He was determined to approach this standard backstage soap opera of mother love and sacrifice with freshness and innovation.

The resultant motion picture, while inevitably dated in story content and the acting styles of some of its performers, continues to impress film scholars with the notable avoidance of clichés in Mamoulian's direction. Visually, the director establishes his scene at the outset, filming on a deserted New York street where abandoned newspaper pages scuttle along with the wind and a stray dog chases a burlesque poster that heralds an imminent parade featuring "KITTY DARLING, QUEEN OF HEARTS." A brass band is then heard, accompanying a procession in which a blowsy-looking Helen Morgan, as Kitty, rides in an open carriage. Then, as band music segues into ragtime, we're inside the burlesque theatre, where Mamoulian reveals its tawdry details, from bored pit musicians to tired and overweight chorus girls. A very-pregnant Kitty passes out onstage and is carried off to her dressing-room sofa, where she gives birth to a daughter, April, while the show goes on.

The movie then quickly encompasses the next seventeen years, with Kitty continuing as a third-rate song-and-dance star, while keeping her growing daughter in the dark with a secluded convent upbringing. But eventually boozy, aging mother and naïve, virginal daughter are reunited, and the latter is faced with the sordid truth, which includes the manipulative comedian Hitch (Fuller Mellish, Jr.), with whom Kitty maintains an unhappy live-in relationship. Subsequently, Hitch makes an unsuccessful play for a repelled April (Joan Peers) who,

surprisingly, joins the burlesque chorus. Despondent, Kitty takes poison and dies in her dressing room, as April goes on in her place. But the girl discovers that applause doesn't fill *her* needs, and she leaves the stage to marry the nice young sailor (Henry Wadsworth) who has been paying her court.

Helen Morgan had won Broadway fame as a star of the stage and nightclub worlds of the Twenties. Between 1929 and 1936, she appeared in only ten films, including both the 1929 and 1936 versions of *Show Boat*, in which she repeated her original stage triumph as the tragic Julie. But her most memorable movie work is as the pathetic heroine of *Applause*, a characterization that, unfortunately, anticipated Morgan's own alcoholic demise twelve years later, at forty-one.

Helen Morgan (at right)

THE TAMING OF THE SHREW

CREDITS

A United Artists Picture. A co-production of the Pickford Corp. and the Elton Corp. Directed by Sam Taylor. Adapted by Sam Taylor from the play by William Shakespeare. Photographed by Karl Struss. Edited by Allen McNeil. Sound by David Forrest. Art Direction by William Cameron Menzies and Laurence Irving. Costumes by Mitchell Leisen. Eight reels.

CAST

Mary Pickford (*Katherine*); Douglas Fairbanks (*Petruchio*); Edwin Maxwell (*Baptista*); Joseph Cawthorn (*Gremio*); Clyde Cook (*Grumio*); Geoffrey Wardwell (*Hortensio*); Dorothy Jordan (*Bianca*).

Mary Pickford and Douglas Fairbanks, Sr., had been America's most popular acting couple since 1920, but it took nearly a decade to unite them in their only joint screen vehicle—produced at a time when their own idealized marriage was, ironically, heading for a breakup. Pickford later admitted that filming *The Taming of the Shrew* with Fairbanks was a painful experience (while praising her former husband's performance).

In 1929, it seemed as though Pickford and Fairbanks could hardly go wrong. His famed series of flamboyant, good-humored swashbucklers had been immensely popular throughout the decade; her reputation as "America's Sweetheart" had prevailed from the long-maturing years of fame as a feisty but adorable "little girl" (well into Pickford's thirties!) into feminine maturity, and an Academy Award for her performance in the talking picture *Coquette* (1928). The pair were literally adored worldwide, and not even the prospect of their making Shakespeare's popular but demanding comedy the vehicle of their co-starring debut seemed chancey. To help matters, this joint Pickford-Fairbanks production (for United Artists distribution) engaged a production crew that was tried and trusted. Its director, Sam Taylor, was well versed in silent-screen comedy and had already guided Mary through 1927's *My Best Girl* and *Coquette*, and had just collaborated with Doug on *The Iron Mask* (1929). Their art director William Cameron Menzies had designed *The Thief of Bagdad* for Fairbanks in 1924, as well as Valentino's *The Eagle* a year later.

And although the prospect of tackling Shakespeare must have seemed initially formidable to Pickford and

Mary Pickford and Douglas Fairbanks

Fairbanks, both had stage-trained voices, the roles of Katherine and Petruchio offered characters compatible with their established screen images, and Sam Taylor would cut and simplify the text (eliminating much of the Bard's subplotting) to suit their talents.

Attired in the rich costumes designed by future-director Mitchell Leisen, with expensive-looking sets built by Menzies and Laurence Irving, and with Karl Struss's accomplished photography to gild their showcase, the Fairbankses finally reached the world's screens, in both talking and—for those theatres as yet acoustically unconverted—silent versions of *The Taming of the Shrew*.

Fairbanks's tongue-in-cheek flair for costume characterization lent itself especially well to the Veronese Petruchio's wife-hunting in Padua, where the wealthy merchant Baptista is anxious to marry off Katherine, the tempestuous older of his two daughters. And how Petruchio meets the challenge of taming this man-hating termagant is the core of Shakespeare's story, rendered believable by a Mary Pickford of almost inexhaustible feist and fury. When this Katherine reasons that the best

way to accede to her groom is by *pretending* to be tamed, a broad end-of-film wink to her sister Bianca (Dorothy Jordan) informs us that her groom is in for a few surprises!

Most contemporary critics received this popularized Shakespearean package with commendable good grace, praising the charm of its stars and Taylor's success in reworking the Bard's rambunctious farce for the pleasure of the Hollywood-oriented cinema masses. Few criticized the stars' obvious vocal limitations, overemphasized histrionics or inexperience as classical performers. And yet the masses stayed away. *The Taming of the Shrew* was not among 1929's box-office winners. An era was ending, both personally and professionally, for two of movieland's holiest icons. With their great years behind them, Mary and Doug would, separately, act in but a handful of indifferently received movies before premature retirement.

As Fairbanks had prophetically remarked to *Shrew*'s associate production designer Laurence Irving, "the romance of filmmaking ends here."